Praise for **This Afterlife**

MW00638769

"Stallings's formal ingenuity lends a music to her philosophically and narratively compelling verse . . . [She crafts] clever yet profound meditations on love, motherhood, language, and time. A particular pleasure is seeing certain personae—Persephone, Daphne, and Alice (of Wonderland)—recur throughout, accompanied by ever-deepening resonances."
  —*The New Yorker*

"Stallings's new book, *This Afterlife: Selected Poems*, is a major event . . . Poems are either memorable or not, and *This Afterlife* is loaded with the real stuff, the right stuff, the kind of lines you remember."
  —Jason Guriel, *Air Mail*

"Technically assured . . . Profound and disturbing . . . [*This Afterlife*] should introduce Stallings's mastery to a wider public."
  —Graeme Richardson, *The Sunday Times* (London)

"One of the . . . most consistently excellent poets writing today . . . Stallings's poems . . . offer us the hard-won fruits of suffering and loss, a wisdom cured in tears."
  —Jeffrey Bilbro, *Plough*

"Rooted in Athens for more than twenty years, the American-born Stallings has not forgotten the song that imbued her earlier work. If anything, her variations on myth and reflections on the modern world around her, with its overlapping crises, have grown at once more intricate and more assured."
  —Boris Dralyuk, *The Times Literary Supplement*

"In the realm of contemporary formal poetry, Stallings is an Olympic-level athlete, and this mid-career retrospective demonstrates how she has been redefining the field for over two decades . . . This new career-spanning collection shows us both Stallings' range and her depth, her intelligence, and her heart."

—**Erica Reid**, *Colorado Review*

"[Stallings's poems] never fail to delight, challenge, and surprise with their dexterity of craft and unexpected, revelatory results . . . Her re-examinations of iconic female figures from antiquity, coupled with often witty, complex explorations of domestic life are testament to her impressive imagination and facility with language—all earning her, to my mind, a rightful place in the feminist authorial pantheon."

—**Michelle Bitting**, *The Rumpus*

This Afterlife

Also by A. E. *Stallings*

Poetry

Archaic Smile

Hapax

Olives

Like

Translation

The Nature of Things by Lucretius

Works and Days by Hesiod

The Battle Between the Frogs and the Mice:
A Tiny Homeric Epic

THIS AFTERLIFE

A. E. STALLINGS

SELECTED POEMS

FARRAR STRAUS GIROUX — NEW YORK

Farrar, Straus and Giroux
120 Broadway, New York 10271

The Library of Congress has cataloged the hardcover edition as follows:
Names: Stallings, A. E. (Alicia Elsbeth), 1968– author.
Title: This afterlife : selected poems / A.E. Stallings.
Description: First edition. | New York : Farrar, Straus and Giroux, 2022. |
   Includes index.
Identifiers: LCCN 2022023796 | ISBN 9780374600693 (hardcover)
Subjects: LCGFT: Poetry.
Classification: LCC PS3569.T3197 T55 2022 | DDC 811/.54—dc23/eng/20220524
LC record available at https://lccn.loc.gov/2022023796

Paperback ISBN: 978-0-374-60783-8

Designed by Crisis

Our books may be purchased in bulk for promotional,
educational, or business use. Please contact your local
bookseller or the Macmillan Corporate and Premium
Sales Department at 1-800-221-7945, extension 5442, or
by email at MacmillanSpecialMarkets@macmillan.com.

www.fsgbooks.com
www.twitter.com/fsgbooks
www.facebook.com/fsgbooks

10 9 8 7 6 5 4 3 2 1

For **John**, **Jason**, *and* **Atalanta**

Surprised by sunlight, air, this afterlife.

Contents

From *Olives* (2012)

"Lagniappe" of Uncollected Poems (1999-2017)

From

ARCHAIC **SMILE**

(1999)

A Postcard from Greece

Hatched from sleep, as we slipped out of orbit
Round a clothespin curve new-watered with the rain,
I saw the sea, the sky, as bright as pain,
That outer space through which we were to plummet.
No guardrails hemmed the road, no way to stop it,
The only warning, here and there, a shrine:
Some tended still, some antique and forgotten,
Empty of oil, but all were consecrated
To those who lost their wild race with the road
And sliced the tedious sea once, like a knife.
Somehow we struck an olive tree instead.
Our car stopped on the cliff's brow. Suddenly safe,
We clung together, shade to pagan shade,
Surprised by sunlight, air, this afterlife.

Hades Welcomes His Bride

Come now, child, adjust your eyes, for sight
Is here a lesser sense. Here you must learn
Directions through your fingertips and feet
And map them in your mind. I think some shapes
Will gradually appear. The pale things twisting
Overhead are mostly roots, although some worms
Arrive here clinging to their dead. Turn here.
Ah. And in this hall will sit our thrones,
And here you shall be queen, my dear, the queen
Of all men ever to be born. No smile?
Well, some solemnity befits a queen.
These thrones I have commissioned to be made
Are unlike any you imagined; they glow
Of deep-black diamonds and lead, subtler
And in better taste than gold, as will suit
Your timid beauty and pale throat. Come now,
Down these winding stairs, the air more still
And dry and easier to breathe. Here is a room
For your diversions. Here I've set a loom
And silk unravelled from the finest shrouds
And dyed the richest, rarest shades of black.
Such pictures you shall weave! Such tapestries!
For you I chose those three thin shadows there,
And they shall be your friends and loyal maids,
And do not fear from them such gossiping
As servants usually are wont. They have

Not mouth nor eyes and cannot thus speak ill
Of you. Come, come. This is the greatest room;
I had it specially made after great thought
So you would feel at home. I had the ceiling
Painted to recall some evening sky—
But without the garish stars and lurid moon.
What? That stark shape crouching in the corner?
Sweet, that is to be our bed. Our bed.
Ah! Your hand is trembling! I fear
There is, as yet, too much pulse in it.

Persephone Writes a
Letter to Her Mother

First—hell is not so far underground—
My hair gets tangled in the roots of trees
& I can just make out the crunch of footsteps,
The pop of acorns falling, or the chime
Of a shovel squaring a fresh grave or turning
Up the tulip bulbs for separation.
Day & night, creatures with no legs
Or too many, journey to hell and back.
Alas, the burrowing animals have dim eyesight.
They are useless for news of the upper world.
They say the light is "loud" (their figures of speech
All come from sound; their hearing is acute).

The dead are just as dull as you would imagine.
They evolve like the burrowing animals—losing their sight.
They may roam abroad sometimes—but just at night—
They can only tell me if there was a moon.
Again and again, moth-like, they are duped
By any beckoning flame—lamps and candles.
They come back startled & singed, sucking their fingers,
Happy the dirt is cool and dense and blind.
They are silly & grateful and don't remember anything.
I have tried to tell them stories, but they cannot attend.
They pester you like children for the wrong details—
How long were his fingernails? Did she wear shoes?

ARCHAIC SMILE

How much did they eat for breakfast? What is snow?
And then they pay no attention to the answers.

My husband, bored with their babbling, neither listens nor speaks.
But here there is no fodder for small talk.
The weather is always the same. Nothing happens.
(Though at times I feel the trees, rocking in place
Like grief, clenching the dirt with tortuous toes.)
There is nothing to eat here but raw beets & turnips.
There is nothing to drink but mud-filtered rain.
Of course, no one goes hungry or toils, however many—
(The dead breed like the bulbs of daffodils—
Without sex or seed—all underground—
Yet no race has such increase. Worse than insects!)

I miss you and think about you often.
Please send flowers. I am forgetting them.
If I yank them down by the roots, they lose their petals
And smell of compost. Though I try to describe
Their color and fragrance, no one here believes me.
They think they are the same thing as mushrooms.
Yet no dog is so loyal as the dead,
Who have no wives or children and no lives,
No motives, secret or bare, to disobey.
Plus, my husband is a kind, kind master;
He asks nothing of us, nothing, nothing at all—
Thus fall changes to winter, winter to fall,
While we learn idleness, a difficult lesson.

He does not understand why I write letters.
He says that you will never get them. True—
Mulched-leaf paper sticks together, then rots;
No ink but blood, and it turns brown like the leaves.
He found my stash of letters, for I had hid it,
Thinking he'd be angry. But he never angers.
He took my hands in his hands, my shredded fingers
Which I have sliced for ink, thin paper cuts.
My effort is futile, he says, and doesn't forbid it.

Eurydice's Footnote

. . . a single Hellenistic poem, on which Virgil and Ovid drew freely . . .
made a vitally important change by turning the recovery of Eurydice,
whether complete or temporary, into a tragic loss.
—C. M. Bowra, *The Classical Quarterly*, 1952

Love, then, always was a matter of revision
As reality, to poet or to politician
Is but the first rough draft of history or legend.
So your artist's eye, a sharp and perfect prism,
Refracts discrete components of a beauty
To fix them in some still more perfect order.
(I say this on the other side of order
Where things can be re-invented no longer.)

Still I recall, at times, the critical moment
When nothing was so difficult as you had wanted,
And knowing my love would grow back for you like any crop,
You turned your head, an inhospitable, cold planet
(Your eyes—flash, flash, like sickles)—
How the sun grew far away again and small
As a red eye at the telescope's far tapering.
Life proved fickle as any lover.

I still imagine your explanation, were it to come,
As in some catalogued and hardbound learned journal
Speaking with 100 iron tongues of respected criticism:

Disappointment in the end was more aesthetic
Than any merely felicitous resolution.

How the Demons Were Assimilated
& Became Productive Citizens

The demons were more beautiful than the angels.
They had no qualms about plastic surgery.
They took to wearing black: didn't show dirt
In the city like Innocence, which anyway
Couldn't be worn between Labor Day and Easter.
They tired of grudging angels their gilded hair
& had theirs done. Their complexions were so pale
The blond looked natural, only more so.
They shrunk their wings into fashionable tattoos
So cashmere suits draped better from their shoulders.
Elocution lessons turned hisses to lisps.

The demons converted. They became Episcopalian,
Name-dropped high-ups in the Company of Heaven.
As for Evil, it became too much trouble:
The demons started to shirk the menial jobs
Which, like good deeds, took one among the poor,
And bruised the manicure of rose-petal nails.
They preferred to stand by & watch Evil happen,
Or offended by odors & noise, even turned away.

They had become so beautiful, even the angels
(Who never looked in mirrors to comb their hair,
Afraid to be called vain, & never bought clothes
Since the old ones didn't wear out, just got shabby)
Left the lovely demons to languish, dropping all charges
On the spoiled creatures. They were that good.

Cardinal Numbers

Mrs. Cardinal is dead:
All that remains—a beak of red,
And, fanned across the pavement slab,
Feathers, drab.

Remember how we saw her mate
In the magnolia tree of late,
Glowing, in the faded hour,
A scarlet flower,

And knew, from his nagging sound,
His wife foraged on the ground,
As camouflaged, as he (to us)
Conspicuous?

One of us remarked, with laughter,
It was her safety he looked after,
On the watch, from where he sat,
For dog or cat

(For being lately married we
Thought we had the monopoly,
Nor guessed a bird so glorious
Uxorious).

Of course, the reason that birds flocked
To us: we kept the feeder stocked.
And there are cats (why mince words)
Where there are birds.

A possum came when dusk was grey,
And so tidied the corpse away,
While Mr. Cardinal at dawn
Carried on,

As if to say, he doesn't blame us,
Our hospitality is famous.
If other birds still want to visit,
Whose fault is it?

A Lament for the Dead
Pets of Our Childhood

Even now I dream of rabbits murdered
By loose dogs in the dark, the saved-up voice
Spilt on that last terror, or the springtime
Of lost baby rabbits, grey and blind
As moles, that slipped from birth and from the nest
Into a grey, blind rain, became the mud.
And still I gather up their shapes in dreams,
Those poor, leftover Easter eggs, all grey.

That's how we found out death: the strangled bird
Undone by a toy hung in his cage,
The foundlings that would never last the night,
Be it pigeon, crippled snake, the kitten
Whose very fleas forsook it in the morning
While we nursed a hangover of hope.

After the death of pets, dolls lay too still
And wooden in the cradle, sister, after
We learned death: not hell, no ghosts or angels,
But a cold thing in the image of a warm thing,
Limp as sleep without the twitch of dreams.

Homecoming

for Ashley and Shelby

It was as if she pulled a thread,
Each time he saw her, that unravelled
All the distance he had travelled
To sleep at home in his own bed,
Or sit together in a room
Spinning yarns of monsters, wars,
Hours counted by the chores.
He loved to watch her at the loom:
The fluent wrists, the liquid motion
Of small tasks not thought about,
The shuttle leaping in and out,
Dolphins sewing the torn ocean.

Consolation for Tamar

on the occasion of her breaking an ancient pot

You know I am no archaeologist, Tamar,
And that to me it is all one dust or another.
Still, it must mean something to survive the weather
Of the Ages—earthquake, flood, and war—

Only to shatter in your very hands.
Perhaps it was gravity, or maybe fated—
Although I wonder if it had not waited
Those years in drawers, aeons in distant lands,

And in your fingers' music, just a little
Was emboldened by your blood, and so forgot
That it was not a rosebud, but a pot,
And, trying to unfold for you, was brittle.

Apollo Takes Charge of His Muses

They sat there, nine women, much the same age,
The same poppy-red hair, and similar complexions
Freckling much the same in the summer glare,
The same bright eyes of green melting to blue
Melting to golden brown, they sat there,
Nine women, all of them very quiet, one,
Perhaps, was looking at her nails, one plaited
Her hair in narrow strands, one stared at a stone,
One let fall a mangled flower from her hands,
All nine of them very quiet, and the one who spoke
Said, softly:

"Of course he was very charming, and he smiled,
Introduced himself and said he'd heard good things,
Shook hands all round, greeted us by name,
Assured us it would all be much the same,
Explained his policies, his few minor suggestions
Which we would please observe. He looked forward
To working with us. Wouldn't it be fun? Happy
To answer any questions. Any questions? But
None of us spoke or raised her hand, and questions
There were none; what has poetry to do with reason
Or the sun?"

Crazy to Hear the Tale Again
(The Fall of Troy)

. . . ferit aurea sidera clamor
—Virgil, *Aeneid* 2.488

The stars were golden! Golden as the fire—
We had seen nothing like it, ah, but then
Such things that night, we'll not see such again.
But stars, we'd thought, were purer, somehow: higher—

And yet it seemed a blush that turned them gold.
What once was chill alike to joy or harm
That one strange night seemed somehow to grow warm
And dashed the hopes long cherished by the Old

That Nature was a white and mindless thing
Of perfect mathematical design
As snowflakes are, as blameless and as fine
(For lo, the stars grew gold and maddening).

Yes, there were horrors hinted in that night.
I thought a veil was parted from my eyes
And thought I saw our gods, of monstrous size,
Splash barefoot in our blood, and with delight.

Medea, Homesick

How many gifted witches, young and fair,
Have flunked, been ordinary, left the back-
Stooping study of their art, black
Or white, for love, that sudden foreigner?
Because chalk-fingered Wisdom streaks the hair,
Because the flame that flaps upon its wick
Rubrics the eye, I left behind the book
And washed my hands of ink, my homeland, my father.
But beauty doesn't travel well: the ocean,
Sun-strong years. The charms I knew by rote,
Irregular as verbs, decline to charm.
I cannot spell the simplest old potion
I learned for love. As for the antidote,
He discovered it himself, and is past harm.

The Wife of the Man of Many Wiles

Believe what you want to. Believe that I wove,
If you wish, twenty years, and waited, while you
Were knee-deep in blood, hip-deep in goddesses.

I've not much to show for twenty years' weaving—
I have but one half-finished cloth at the loom.
Perhaps it's the lengthy, meticulous grieving.

Explain how you want to. Believe I unravelled
At night what I stitched in the slow siesta,
How I kept them all waiting for me to finish,

The suitors, you call them. Believe what you want to.
Believe that they waited for me to finish,
Believe I beguiled them with nightly un-doings.

Believe what you want to. That they never touched me.
Believe your own stories, as you would have me do,
How you only survived by the wise infidelities.

Believe that each day you wrote me a letter
That never arrived. Kill all the damn suitors
If you think it will make you feel better.

Tour of the Labyrinth

And this is where they kept it, though their own,
Hungry in the dark beneath the stair,
And fed it apple cores, the odd soup bone,
And virgins with their torches of gold hair.

When howls were heard, they claimed it was the earth,
Subduction of a continental plate,
Put down their sherry glasses with thin mirth,
Excused themselves, and said that it was late.

But when the earth *did* make a mooing sound,
Stones that had been stacked into the wall
Knelt to the embracing of the ground.
Amid the gravity that struck them all

No one thought to go unlock the door.
Archaeologists, amazed to find
A skeleton they were not looking for,
Said it was the only of its kind.

They've unravelled the last days of the thing:
It lived a while on rats and bitumen,
And played with its one toy, a ball of string,
To puzzle out the darkness it was in.

Daphne

Poet, Singer, Necromancer—
I cease to run. I halt you here,
Pursuer, with an answer:

Do what you will.
What blood you've set to music I
Can change to chlorophyll,

And root myself, and with my toes
Wind to subterranean streams.
Through solid rock my strength now grows.

Such now am I, I cease to eat,
But feed on flashes from your eyes;
Light, to my new cells, is meat.

Find then, when you seize my arm
That xylem thickens in my skin
And there are splinters in my charm.

I may give in; I do not lose.
Your hot stare cannot stop my shivering,
With delight, if I so choose.

Arachne Gives Thanks to Athena

It is no punishment. They are mistaken—
The brothers, the father. My prayers were answered.
I was all fingertips. Nothing was perfect:
What I had woven, the moths will have eaten;
At the end of my rope was a noose's knot.

Now it's no longer the thing, but the pattern,
And that will endure, even though webs be broken.

I, if not beautiful, am beauty's maker.
Old age cannot rob me, nor cowardly lovers.
The moon once pulled blood from me. Now I pull silver.
Here are the lines I pulled from my own belly—
Hang them with rainbows, ice, dewdrops, darkness.

The Mistake

The mistake was light and easy in my hand,
A seed meant to be borne upon the wind.
I did not have to bury it or throw,
Just open up my hand and let it go.

The mistake was dry and small and without weight,
A breeze quickly snatched it from my sight,
And even had I wanted to prevent,
Nobody could tell me where it went.

I did not think on the mistake again,
Until the spring came, soft, and full of rain,
And in the yard such dandelions grew
That bloomed and closed, and opened up, and blew.

The Tantrum

Struck with grief you were, though only four,
The day your mother cut her mermaid hair
And stood, a stranger, smiling at the door.

They frowned, tsk-tsked your willful, cruel despair,
When you slunk beneath the long piano strings
And sobbed until your lungs hiccupped for air,

Unbribable with curses, cake, playthings.
You mourned a mother now herself no more,
But brave and fashionable. The golden rings

That fringed her naked neck, whom were they for?
Not you, but for the world, now in your place,
A full eclipse. You wept down on the floor;

She wept up in her room. They told you this:
That she could grow it back, and just as long,
They told you, lying always about loss,

For you know she never did. And they were wrong.

Fishing

The two of them stood in the middle water,
The current slipping away, quick and cold,
The sun slow at his zenith, sweating gold,
Once, in some sullen summer of father and daughter.
Maybe he regretted he had brought her—
She'd rather have been elsewhere, her look told—
Perhaps a year ago, but now too old.
Still, she remembered lessons he had taught her:
To cast towards shadows, where the sunlight fails
And fishes shelter in the undergrowth.
And when the unseen strikes, how all else pales
Beside the bright-dark struggle, the rainbow wroth,
Life and death weighed in the shining scales,
The invisible line pulled taut that links them both.

Study in White

A friend, an artist, phoned me up and said,
What shall I do for flesh? And what for bone?
All has some white, and the best white is lead.

But lead gets in the flesh and in the bone,
And if you are a woman, in the child
You bear years hence, and I know, have read

That you may use titanium or zinc,
Not poisonous, but you may be reviled
Because you lack the seriousness bred

For art in men—or how else could you think
Of compromise in this. And I own
I've tried them both, but the best white is lead

For making up the colors bold and mild,
Conceiving still lifes, matching tone with tone
To reproduce the spectra of the dead.

And I have stood for hours at the sink
Scrubbing white from hands until they bled.
And still my hands are stained, and still I think—
O flesh and blood—but the best white is lead.

The Machines Mourn the Passing of People

We miss the warmth of their clumsy hands,
The oil of their fingers, the cleansing of use
That warded off dust, and the warm abuse
Lavished upon us as reprimands.

We were kicked like dogs when we were broken,
But we did not whimper. We gritted our cogs—
An honor it was to be treated as dogs,
To incur such warm words roughly spoken,

The way that they pleaded with us if we balked—
"Come on, come on" in a hoarse whisper
As they would urge a reluctant lover—
The feel of their warm breath when they talked!

How could we guess they would ever be gone?
We are shorn now of tasks, and the lovely work—
Not toiling, not spinning—like lilies that shirk—
Like the brash dandelions that savage the lawn.

The air now is silent of curses or praise.
Jilted, abandoned to hells of what weather,
Left to our own devices forever,
We watch the sun rust at the end of its days.

The Man Who Wouldn't
Plant Willow Trees

Willows are messy trees. Hair in their eyes,
They weep like women after too much wine
And not enough love. They litter a lawn with leaves
Like the butts of regrets smoked down to the filter.

They are always out of kilter. Thirsty as drunks,
They'll sink into a sewer with their roots.
They have no pride. There's never enough sorrow.
A breeze threatens and they shake with sobs.

Willows are slobs, and must be cleaned up after.
They'll bust up pipes just looking for a drink.
Their fingers tremble, but make wicked switches.
They claim they are sorry, but they whisper it.

From

HAPAX

(2006)

Aftershocks

We are not in the same place after all.
The only evidence of the disaster,
Mapping out across the bedroom wall,
Tiny cracks still fissuring the plaster—
A new cartography for us to master,
In whose legend we read where we are bound:
Terra infirma, a stranger land, and vaster.
Or have we always stood on shaky ground?
The moment keeps on happening: a sound.
The floor beneath us swings, a pendulum
That clocks the heart, the heart so tightly wound,
We fall mute, as when two lovers come
To the brink of the apology, and halt,
Each standing on the wrong side of the fault.

The Dollhouse

There in the attic of forgotten shapes
(Old coats in plastic, hatboxes, fur capes
Amongst the smells of mothballs and cigars),
I saw the dollhouse of our early years,
With which my mother and my aunt had played,
And later where my sister and I made
The towering grown-up hours to smile and pass:
The little beds, the tinfoil looking glass,
Bookcases stamped in ink upon the walls,
Mismatched chairs where sat the jointed dolls,
The clock whose face, no larger than a dime,
Had, for all these years, kept the same time.
I remembered how we set the resin food
Atop a table of stained balsa wood,
The shiny turkey hollow to the tap,
The cherry pie baked in a bottle cap.
Now it is time to go to sleep, we spoke,
Parroting the talk of older folk,
And laid the dolls out fully clothed in bed
After their teeth were brushed, and prayers were said,
And flipped the switch on the low-wattage sun.
But in the night we'd have something break in,
Kidnap the baby or purloin the pie—
A tiger, maybe, or a passerby—
Just to make something happen, to move the story.
The dolls awoke, alarmed, took inventory.

If we made something happen every day,
Or night, it was the game we knew to play,
Not realizing then how lives accrue,
With interest, the smallest things we do.

Lovejoy Street

The house where we were happy,
Perhaps it's standing still
On the wrong side of the railroad tracks
Half-way down the hill.

Perhaps new people live there
Who think the street name quaint,
And watch the dogwood petals shiver
Down like flakes of paint.

Perhaps they hold each other
When the train goes railing by,
Shaking up the windowpanes
And dressing down the sky.

And perhaps it strikes them rich
When spring is making shift,
To find the bank in blooming pink
Where we had planted thrift.

Perhaps they reap our roses
In an antique jelly jar.
And maybe they are happy there,
And do not know they are.

Sine Qua Non

Your absence, father, is nothing. It is naught—
The factor by which nothing will multiply,
The gap of a dropped stitch, the needle's eye
Weeping its black thread. It is the spot
Blindly spreading behind the looking glass.
It is the startled silences that come
When the refrigerator stops its hum,
And crickets pause to let the winter pass.

Your absence, father, is nothing—for it is
Omega's long last O, memory's elision,
The fraction of impossible division,
The element I move through, emptiness,
The void stars hang in, the interstice of lace,
The zero that still holds the sum in place.

Last Will

What he *really* wanted, she confesses,
Was to be funnelled into shells and shot
Across a dove-field. Only, she could not—

The kick of shotguns knocks her over. Well,
I say, he'd understand. It doesn't matter
What becomes of atoms, how they scatter.

The priest reads the committal, something short.
We drop the little velvet pouch of dust
Down a cylindrical hole bored in the clay—

And one by one, the doves descend, ash-gray,
Softly as cinders on the parking lot,
And silence sounds its deafening report.

Arrowhead Hunting

The land is full of what was lost. What's hidden
Rises to the surface after rain
In new-ploughed fields, and fields stubbled again:
The clay sherds, foot and lip, that heaped the midden,

And here and there a blade or flakes of blade,
A patient art, knapped from a core of flint,
Most broken, few as coins new from the mint,
Perfect, shot through time as through a glade.

You cannot help but think how they were lost:
The quarry, fletched shaft in its flank, the blood
Whose trail soon vanished in the antlered wood,
Not just the meat, but what the weapon cost—

O hapless hunter, though your aim was true—
The spooked hart, wounded, fleeting in its fear—
And the sharpness honed with longing, year by year
Buried deeper, found someday, but not by you.

Ubi Sunt *Lament for the Eccentric Museums of My Childhood*

Orphaned oddments crammed
in university base-
ments, in corridors

of state capitols,
identified by jaundiced
index cards, I think

about you now—where
have the curators of new
collections stashed you?—

a clutch of geodes
cracked like dragon eggs in mid-
metamorphosis,

coins trite from dead hands,
the two-headed calf floating
in amniotics

of formaldehyde.
Where is Doc Holliday's old
dentist chair? the lone

token mummy, sans
sarcophagus, all unrav-
elling bandages?

(On dares, we looked up
his double-barrelled nose at
cocked eternity.)

Is he under wraps
now, x-rayed, with a puffed-up
provenance, rewound,

educational?
Curators, where are the lost
curiosities,

stranded at random
on Time's littered littoral?
Why, we used to muse,

did this thing, not that,
survive its gone moment—how
are they filed away?

Thyme

I have some of it still,
We gathered on the hill,
In an empty glass, the bunch of wild thyme,

Faded now, and dried,
But in which yet abide
Some purple, a smell of summer in its prime,

When we stopped the car
Bought honey in a jar
At a roadside stand. It makes me think about

The theft of bloom, the sting,
A swiftness on the wing,
Things that sweetness cannot be without.

The Charioteer

Delphi Museum

Lips apart, dry eyes steady,
He stands forever at the ready,

Fingers open, sensitive
To the horses' take and give

(Although no single steed remains
At the end of tangled reins).

It is as if we are not here—
The way the patient charioteer

Looks beyond us, into space,
For some sign to begin the race.

He has stared down centuries.
No wave from us, no sudden breeze,

Will trick him now to a false start.
He has learned the racer's art

To stand watchful at the gate,
Empty out the mind, and wait.

As long as it is in our power
We gaze—maybe for half an hour—

Before we turn from him to go.
Outside, the hills begin to glow,

Burnished by a brazen sun
Whose course now is almost run.

We shiver, and around us feel
Vanished horses plunge and wheel.

Asphodel

after the words of Penny Turner, Nymphaion, Greece

Our guide turned in her saddle, broke the spell:
"You ride now through a field of asphodel,
The flower native to the plains of hell.

Across just such a field the pale shade came
Of proud Achilles, who had preferred a name
And short life to a long life without fame,

And summoned by Odysseus he gave
This wisdom, 'Better by far to be a slave
Among the living, than great among the grave.'

I used to wonder, how did such a bloom
Become associated with the tomb?
Then one evening, walking through the gloom,

I noticed a strange fragrance. It was sweet,
Like honey—but with hints of rotting meat.
An army of them bristled at my feet."

An Ancient Dog Grave, Unearthed During Construction of the Athens Metro

It is not the curled-up bones, nor even the grave
That stops me, but the blue beads on the collar
(Whose leather has long gone the way of hides)—
The ones to ward off evil. A careful master
Even now protects a favorite, just so.
But what evil could she suffer after death?
I picture the loyal companion, bereaved of her master,
Trotting the long, dark way that slopes to the river,
Nearly trampled by all the nations marching down,
One war after another, flood or famine,
Her paws sucked by the thick, caliginous mud,
Deep as her dewclaws, near the riverbank.
In the press for the ferry, who will lift her into the boat?
Will she cower under the pier and be forgotten,
Forever howling and whimpering, tail tucked under?
What stranger pays her passage? Perhaps she swims,
Dog-paddling the current of oblivion.
A shake as she scrambles ashore sets the beads jingling.
And then, that last, tense moment—touching noses
Once, twice, three times, with unleashed Cerberus.

The Modern Greek for "Nightmare" Is Ephialtes

I think, what brought you to this pass?
Heroes lie thick, anonymous,

Blurred with honorable mention
In mass graves of fine intention,

And yet even now dreams yield
On their unequal battlefield

Betrayal's still familiar face,
The name that nothing can erase,

Not even final victory.
Sleep has no sense of history:

Even now I lose the day,
Always look the other way,

While old treachery awaits
The heart's warm springs, its hot gates.

Dead Language Lesson

They lift their half-closed eyes out of the grammar.

What is the object of love? *You,*
Singular. The subject? *I.*

Aeneas has nothing to say for himself.
Even the boys confess that he
Didn't intend to come back, the girls
Already know the tale by heart.

They wheedle me for tangents, for
Anything not in a book,
Even though it's all from books:
The many-wiled Penelope,
Orpheus struck dumb with hindsight.

I confiscate a note in which
The author writes, "who do you love?"—
An agony past all correction.

I think, as they wait for the bell,
Blessed are the young for whom
All languages are dead: the girl
Who twines her golden hair, like Circe,
Turning glib boys into swine.

First Love: A Quiz

He came up to me:
- a. in his souped-up Camaro
- b. to talk to my skinny best friend
- c. and bumped my glass of wine so I wore the ferrous stain on my sleeve
- d. from the ground, in a lead chariot drawn by a team of stallions black as crude oil and breathing sulfur; at his heart, he sported a tiny golden arrow

He offered me:
- a. a ride
- b. dinner and a movie, with a wink at the cliché
- c. an excuse not to go back alone to the apartment with its sink of dirty knives
- d. a narcissus with a hundred dazzling petals that breathed a sweetness as cloying as decay

I went with him because:
- a. even his friends told me to beware
- b. I had nothing to lose except my virginity
- c. he placed his hand in the small of my back and I felt the tread of honeybees
- d. he was my uncle, the one who lived in the half-finished basement, and he took me by the hair

The place he took me to:

 a. was dark as my shut eyes

 b. and where I ate bitter seed and became ripe

 c. and from which my mother would never take me wholly back,
    though she wept and walked the earth and made the bearded
    ears of barley wither on their stalks and the blasted flowers drop
    from their sepals

 d. is called by some men hell and others love

 e. all of the above

"To Speke of Wo That Is in Mariage"

"It is a choreography as neat
As two folding up a laundered sheet,
The way we dance around what we would say:
Approach, meet, touch, then slowly back away.

To sweep is to know what gathers there
Beneath the bed: sloughed cells, lost strands of hair.
To wash clothes well is to take certain pains:
The sad and sordid stories of the stains.

Although my anger may be slow to boil,
I have the smoking point of olive oil.
Every time I wield a knife, I cry.
He has become the onion of my eye.

I dwell upon, it's true. He will not linger.
When I grow cold, the ring slips from my finger."

Fragment

The glass does not break because it is glass,
Said the philosopher. The glass could stay
Unbroken forever, shoved back in a dark closet,
Slowly weeping itself, a colorless liquid.
The glass breaks because somebody drops it
From a height—a grip stunned open by bad news
Or laughter. A giddy sweep of grand gesture
Or fluttering nerves might knock it off the table—
Or perhaps wine emptied from it, into the blood,
Has numbed the fingers. It breaks because it falls
Into the arms of the earth—that grave attraction.
It breaks because it meets the floor's surface,
Which is solid and does not give. It breaks because
It is dropped, and falls hard, because it hits
Bottom, and because nobody catches it.

Evil Eye

"Yes, it's on you," Kalliópe frowns,
Dribbling amber beads of olive oil
Down thick fingers into the water glass
Where they amass
In one big cyclops-blob, and do not scatter.

Something, it seems, always *is* the matter.
Vague pains, or clumsy accidents, a dim
Nimbus on my head, a personal cloud.
Perhaps she *is* endowed
With second sight. I'm lifted by a loss

As she thumbs my forehead with a cross;
Anointed, for a moment, I forget
The failed rehearsals of a mirth, and grief
Floods me like relief.
Yes, something's wrong, something she can *see*.

Even you glance differently at me
For half a second, though we do not believe
In village superstition. Still, we ask,
And she performs the task:
I always have it, and she always takes

It off me (which gives her stomachaches).
And we are grateful, but do not offer thanks—
That would undo it somehow. We walk out
Like shadows of a doubt
Into the changed look of the afternoon.

Empty Icon Frame

Glykophilousa, Virgin of Tenderness

The preciousness was mortal: pigment and wood—
    Dissolved to dust, they leave behind
        Vacancies the mind
Fills in, imagining the faces good

And sorrowful: the mother's kiss, the child
    Oddly wizened, his grave gesture,
        His gaze nailed to the future,
His lips slightly curved as if they smiled.

We know the archetype, so we can see
    From outlines, the old attitudes,
        The chroma that eludes
Us now, expanse of lapis lazuli

Lavished only on her modest raiment,
    Those heaven-saturated blues,
        Costliest of hues—
Spending in itself a kind of payment—

And haloes gently brushed in powdered gold
    Ruddy and rich, which this carapace
        Of silver would replace
In time—every flowing lap and fold

Of garment, where his phantom small hand clings,
        Hammered now in stiff relief
            And gilded in gold leaf,
Glinting like armor—the metal renderings

Defining absence, as if its silhouette meant
        That somehow soft flesh could be thirled
           Forever to the world,
Or Love outlast its glittering revetment.

FROM *Exile: Picture Postcards*

iii. Bouzouki

After five years here, I understand
Most of the sung words, recognize the tune,
But there's an element I'll never get,

That isn't born in me. The way they play—
One manages to hold his cigarette
Between two fingers on his strumming hand,

Takes drags between his solos—and then soon
How something changes: a woman starts to sway
Around an absent center—ancient wrongs

Cherished. The cigarette gives up its ghost.
The music drives now. Someone makes a toast
As suddenly the melody arrives

At minor,
            Asia Minor,
                        in whose songs

The hands of lovers always rhyme with knives.

Explaining an Affinity for Bats

That they are only glimpsed in silhouette,
And seem something else at first—a swallow—
And move like new tunes, difficult to follow,
Staggering towards an obstacle they yet
Avoid in a last-minute pirouette,
Somehow telling solid things from hollow,
Sounding out how high a space, or shallow,
Revising into deepening violet.

That they sing—not the way the songbird sings
(Whose song is rote, to ornament, finesse)—
But travel by a sort of song that rings
True not in utterance, but harkenings,
Who find their way by calling into darkness
To hear their voice bounce off the shape of things.

Another Lullaby
for Insomniacs

Sleep, she will not linger:
She turns her moon-cold shoulder.
With no ring on her finger,
You cannot hope to hold her.

She turns her moon-cold shoulder
And tosses off the cover.
You cannot hope to hold her:
She has another lover.

She tosses off the cover
And lays the darkness bare.
She has another lover,
Her heart is otherwhere.

She lays the darkness bare.
You slowly realize
Her heart is otherwhere.
There's distance in her eyes.

You slowly realize
That she will never linger,
With distance in her eyes
And no ring on her finger.

Lullaby Near the Railroad Tracks

Go back to sleep. The hour is small.
       A freight train between stations
Shook you out of sleep with all
       Its lonely ululations.

Through the stillness, while you slumber,
       They trundle down the track,
Lugging cattle, coal, and lumber,
       Crying, "alack, alack."

It's cheap to pay the engineer:
       The moon's a shiny dime.
Shut your eyes and you will hear
       The Doppler shift of time.

The hour is small. Resume your rest.
       Tomorrow will be kinder.
Here comes a freight train nosing west,
       Pulling the dawn behind her.

Song for the Women Poets

Sing, sing, because you can.
Descend in murk and pitch.
Double-talk the ferryman
And three-throated bitch.

Sing before the king and queen,
Make the grave to grieve,
Till Persephone weeps kerosene
And wipes it on her sleeve.

And she will grant you your one wish:
To fetch across a river
Black and sticky as licorice
The one you lost forever.

Don't look back. But no one heeds.
You glance down in the water.
The image drowning in the weeds
Could be your phantom daughter.

And part of you leaves Tartarus,
But part stays there to dwell—
You who are both Orpheus
And She he left in Hell.

Jet Lag

Oriented, suddenly Aurora,
I rise without alarm in the random dark,
Already full of purpose, without coffee
Or tea, to the cat's delight, revving her pleasure.

Breakfast is a poem, light, in good measure,
A grapefruit split to reveal the spokes and rays
Of the sunburst wheels on a golden chariot.
I dress, I shake the dewdrops from tips of my tresses.

It is as if I can hear them, imagined horses,
Astir in the stable, fogging the air with their breath,
Snug under blankets, awaiting the curry comb
And oats, ready to set out over the hill,

Over the sleeping city, over the sill
Of the sea, islands dribbled like pancake batter,
Knowing where I am is always East,
Always ahead of the day that's going to matter.

Clean Monday

for Anastasi

Other kites already patched the sky,
As if the clouds were moored with so much string.
To fly a kite seemed like an easy thing.
We fastened on the tail, perhaps awry.

Your nephew gave our offering to the breeze.
It lurched aloft, wagged side to side, and stooped,
And, in an angry handwriting, it looped
Until it suicided in the trees.

An hour to retrieve and fix the craft.
Your nephew strayed away to other games.
We untied knots, and called each other names,
And realized our pettiness, and laughed.

We wrestled with the angel of the air
Until we got his blessing, and the kite
Reared up against the string with all its might,
And your nephew sprinted back to clap and stare.

Then, "Let me hold it please!" he wheedled me.
"But with both hands," I said. And he, "I will."
For a moment he was sailing standing still,
Then in his joy, forgot, and set it free.

Prelude

Lately, at the beginning of concerts when
The first-chair violin
Plays the A four-forty and the bows
Go whirring about the instruments like wings
Over unfingered strings,
The cycling fifths, spectral arpeggios,

As the oboe lights the pure torch of the note,
Something in my throat
Constricts, and tears are startled to my eyes
Helplessly. And lately when I stand
Torn ticket in my hand
In the foyers of museums I surprise

You with a quaver in my rote reply—
Again I overbrim
And corners of the room go prismed, dim.
You'd like to think that it is Truth and Art
That I am shaken by,
So that I must discharge a freighted heart;

But it is not when cellos shoulder the tune,
Nor changing of the key
Nor resolution of disharmony
That makes me almost tremble, and it is not
The ambered afternoon
Slanting through motes of dust a painter caught

Four hundred years ago as someone stands
Opening the blank
Future like a letter in her hands.
It is not masterpieces of first rank,
Not something made
By once-warm fingers, nothing painted, played.

No, no. It is something else. It is something raw
That suddenly falls
Upon me at the start, like loss or awe—
The vertigo of possibility—
The pictures I don't see,
The open strings, the perfect intervals.

Ultrasound

What butterfly—
Brain, soul, or both—
Unfurls here, pallid
As a moth?

(Listen, here's
Another ticker,
Counting under
Mine, and quicker.)

In this cave
What flickers fall,
Adumbrated
On the wall?—

Spine like beads
Strung on a wire,
Abacus
Of our desire,

Moon-face where
Two shadows rhyme,
Two moving hands
That tell the time.

I am the room
The future owns,
The darkness where
It grows its bones.

From

OLIVES

(2012)

Olives

Sometimes a craving comes for salt, not sweet,
For fruits that you can eat
Only if pickled in a vat of tears—
A rich and dark and indehiscent meat
Clinging tightly to the pit—on spears

Of toothpicks maybe, drowned beneath a tide
Of vodka and vermouth,
Rocking at the bottom of a wide,
Shallow, long-stemmed glass, and gentrified,
Or rustic, on a plate cracked like a tooth,

A miscellany of the humble hues
Eponymously drab—
Brown greens and purple browns, the blacks and blues
That chart the slow chromatics of a bruise—
Washed down with swigs of barrel wine that stab

The palate with pine-sharpness. They recall
The harvest and its toil,
The nets spread under silver trees that foil
The blue glass of the heavens in the fall—
Daylight packed in treasuries of oil,

Paradigmatic summers that decline
Like singular archaic nouns, the troops
Of hours in retreat. These fruits are mine—
Small bitter drupes
Full of the golden past and cured in brine.

Jigsaw Puzzle

First, the four corners,
Then the flat edges.
Assemble the lost borders,
Walk the dizzy ledges,

Hoard one color—try
To make it all connected—
The water and the deep sky
And the sky reflected.

Absences align
And lock shapes into place,
And random forms combine
To make a tree, a face.

Slowly you restore
The fractured world and start
To re-create an afternoon before
It fell apart:

Here is summer, here is blue,
Here two lovers kissing,
And here the nothingness shows through
Where one piece is missing.

Recitative

Every night, we couldn't sleep—
Our upstairs neighbors had to keep
Dropping something down the hall—
A barbell or a bowling ball,

And from the window by the bed—
Scaling sharply in my head—
The alley cats expended breath
In arias of love and death.

Dawn again, across the street,
Jackhammers began to beat
Like hangovers, and you would frown—
That well-built house, why tear it down?

Noon, the radiator grill
Groaned, gave off a lesser chill
So that we could take off our coats.
The pipes coughed to clear their throats.

Our nerves were frayed like ravelled sleeves,
We cherished each our minor griefs
To keep them warm until the night
When it was time again to fight;

But we were young, did not need much
To make us laugh instead, and touch,
And could not hear ourselves above
The arias of death and love.

Sublunary

Midsentence, we remembered the eclipse,
Arguing home through our scant patch of park,
Still warm with barrel wine, when none too soon
We checked the hour by glancing at the moon,
Unphased at first by that old ruined marble
Looming like a monument over the hill,
So brimmed with light it seemed about to spill,

Then, there! We watched the thin edge disappear—
The obvious stole over us like awe
That it was our own silhouette we saw,
Slow perhaps to us moon-gazing here
(Reaching for each other's fingertips)
But sweeping like a wing across that stark
Alien surface at the speed of dark.

The crickets stirred from winter sleep to warble
Something out of time, confused and brief,
The roosting birds sang out in disbelief,
The neighborhood's stray dogs began to bark.
And then the moon was gone, and in its place,
A dim red planet hung just out of reach,
As real as a bitter orange or ripened peach

In the penumbra of a tree. At last
We rose and strolled at a reflective pace

Past the taverna crammed with light and smoke
And people drinking, laughing at a joke,
Unaware that anything had passed
Outside in the night where we delayed
Sheltering in the shadow we had made.

Four Fibs

1

Did
Eve
believe
or grapple
over the apple?
Eavesdropping Adam heard her say
to the snake-oil salesman she was not born yesterday.

2

Miss,
this
is not
Bliss. Wisdom
is not the abyss,
but visceral innocence. Kiss
the windfall of the world, she heard him whisper, or hiss.

3

Not
me,

not me!
cried all three.
"You shall creep the earth.
And you shall labor giving birth.
And as for you, you shall toil and sweat for all you're worth."

4

Cross
your
heart and
hope to die,
stick a needle in
your eye. That is the awful oath
of childhood, chapter and verse, genesis of the lie.

Deus Ex Machina

Because we were good at entanglements, but not
Resolution, and made a mess of plot,
Because there was no other way to fulfill
The ancient prophecy, because the will
Of the gods demanded punishment, because
Neither recognized who the other was,
Because there was no difference between
A tragic ending and a comic scene,
Because the play was running out of time,
Because the mechanism of the sublime
To stay in working order needed using,
Because it was a script not of our choosing,
Because we were actors, because we knew for a fact
We were only actors, because we could not act

Telephonophobia

We joke about it. Really, you're annoyed
To make some call I should make on my own—

It doesn't bite, you say. That isn't true.
We keep it on a leash; it isn't tame.

It stalks us in our sleep. And when at last
Some shy, unbidden happiness arrives

That triggers its alarm, it's not for you.
I bring it to my head, it speaks my name:

Old anger pours like poison in my ear—
Or information, cool as dates on stone,

Rocks in its smooth, black cradle. I avoid
The thing, because it holds what I most fear:

At any hour, the future or the past
Can dial into the room and change our lives.

The Argument

After the argument, all things were strange.
They stood divided by their eloquence
Which had surprised them after so much silence.
Now there were real things to rearrange.
Words betokened deeds, but they were both
Lightened briefly, and they were inclined
To be kind as sometimes strangers can be kind.
It was as if, out of the undergrowth,
They stepped into a clearing and the sun,
Machetes still in hand. Something was done,
But how, they did not fully realize.
Something was beginning. Something would stem
And branch from this one moment. Something made
Them each look up into the other's eyes
Because they both were suddenly afraid
And there was no one now to comfort them.

Burned

You cannot unburn what is burned.
Although you scrape the ruined toast,
You can't go back. It's time you learned

The butter cannot be unchurned,
You can't unmail the morning post,
You cannot unburn what is burned—

The lovers in your youth you spurned,
The bridges charred you needed most.
You can't go back. It's time you learned

Smoke's reputation is well earned,
Not just an acrid, empty boast—
You cannot unburn what is burned.

You longed for home, but while you yearned,
The black ships smoldered on the coast;
You can't go back. It's time you learned

That even if you had returned,
You'd only be a kind of ghost.
You can't go back. It's time you learned

That what is burned is burned is burned.

On Visiting a Borrowed
Country House in Arcadia

for John

To leave the city
Always takes a quarrel. Without warning,
Rancors that have gathered half the morning
Like things to pack, or a migraine, or a cloud,
Are suddenly allowed
To strike. They strike the same place twice.
We start by straining to be nice,
Then say something shitty.

Isn't it funny
How it's what *has* to happen
To make the unseen ivory gates swing open,
The rite we must perform so we can leave?
Always we must grieve
Our botched happiness: we goad
Each other till we pull to the hard shoulder of the road,
Yielding to tears inadequate as money.

But if instead
Of turning back, we drive into the day,
We forget the things we didn't say.
The silence fills with row on row
Of vines or olive trees. The radio

Hums to itself. We make our way between
Saronic blue and hills of glaucous green
And thread

Beyond the legend of the map
Through footnote towns along the coast
That boast
Ruins of no account—a column
More woebegone than solemn—
Men watching soccer at the two cafés,
And half-built lots where dingy sheep still graze.
Climbing into the lap

Of the mountains now, we wind
Around blind, centrifugal turns.
The sun's great warship sinks and burns.
And where the roads without a sign are crossed,
We (inevitably) get lost.
Yet to be lost here
Still feels like being somewhere,
And we find

When we arrive and park,
No one minds that we are late—
There is no one to wait—
Only a bed to make, a suitcase to unpack.
The earth has turned her back
On one yellow middling star
To consider lights more various and far.
The shaggy mountains hulk into the dark

Or loom
Like slow, titanic waves. The cries
Of owls dilate the shadows. Weird harmonics rise
From the valley's distant glow, where coal
Extracted from the lignite mines must roll
On acres of conveyor belts that sing
The Pythagorean music of a string.
A huge grey plume

Of smoke or steam
Towers like the ghost of a monstrous flame
Or giant tree among the trees. And it is all the same—
The power plant, the forest, and the night,
The manmade light.
We are engulfed in an immense
Ancient indifference
That does not sleep or dream.

Call it Nature if you will,
Though everything that is is natural—
The lignite-bearing earth, the factory,
A darkness taller than the sky—
This out-of-doors that wins us our release
And temporary peace—
Not because it is pristine or pretty,
But because it has no pity or self-pity.

Triolet on a Line Apocryphally Ascribed to Martin Luther

Why should the Devil get all the good tunes,
The booze and the neon and Saturday night,
The swaying in darkness, the lovers like spoons?
Why should the Devil get all the good tunes?
Does he hum them to while away sad afternoons,
And the long, lonesome Sundays? Or sing them for spite?
Why should the Devil get all the good tunes,
The booze and the neon and Saturday night?

Two Violins

One was fire-red,
Hand-carved and new—
The local maker pried the wood
From a torn-down church's pew,

The Devil's instrument
Wrenched from the house of God.
It answered merrily and clear
Though my fingering was flawed;

Bright and sharp as a young wine,
They said, but it would mellow,
And that I would grow into it.
The other one was yellow

And nicked down at the chin,
A varnish of Baltic amber,
A one-piece back of tiger maple
And a low, dark timbre.

A century old, they said,
Its sound will never change.
Rich and deep on G and D,
Thin on the upper range—

And how it came from the Old World
Was anybody's guess—
Light as an exile's suitcase,
A belly of emptiness:

That was the one I chose—
Not the one of flame—
And teachers turned in their practiced hands
To see whence the sad notes came.

The Ghost Ship

She plies an inland sea. Dull
With rust, scarred by a jagged reef.
In Cyrillic, on her hull
Is lettered *Grief*.

The dim stars do not signify;
No sonar with its eerie ping
Sounds the depths—she travels by
Dead reckoning.

At her heart is a stopped clock.
In her wake, the hours drag.
There is no port where she can dock,
She flies no flag,

Has no allegiance to a state,
No registry, no harbor berth,
Nowhere to discharge her freight
Upon the earth.

Handbook of the Foley Artist

For the sound of distant thunder,
A father frowning,
For the smack of sarcasm,
Pop of bubblegum;

For a sudden summer downpour,
Sizzle of bacon,
For the sound of somewhere else,
Freight train at 2 A.M.;

For the sound of snoring,
Bees in the lilac bush.
For the sound of insomnia,
Eyelashes against a pillowcase;

For the sea's din,
Blood's hush in the cochlea of the ear,
For the screak of a seagull,
The playground's rusted swing;

For the sound of birth,
The radio between pangs,
For death,
Static of flies;

For dry bones,
Fig trees clattering in the wind,

For the vowel of the wind,
A dog left out in the yard;

Crumple paper
For the fricative of fire;
For the gasp of an opened letter,
Strike a match;

Take the telephone off the hook
For the sound of no answer.
For the sound of a broken heart,
Crack a joke.

Extinction of Silence

That it was shy when alive goes without saying.
We know it vanished at the sound of voices

Or footsteps. It took wing at the slightest noises,
Though it could be approached by someone praying.

We have no recordings of it, though of course
In the basement of the Museum, we have some stuffed

Moth-eaten specimens—the Lesser Ruffed
And Yellow Spotted—filed in narrow drawers.

But its song is lost. If it was related to
A species of Quiet, or of another feather,

No researcher can know. Not even whether
A breeding pair still nests deep in the bayou,

Where legend has it some once common bird
Decades ago was first not seen, not heard.

The Cenotaph

First Cemetery of Athens

The day I went to the First Cemetery
Looking for famous graves, the sky was blue
As wild irises in February
And there were mourners walking two by two
And gravediggers who had folk to bury
Along the cypress-vaulted avenue:
Priests and florists, all that's understood
In the solemn bustle of death's livelihood.

I came there seeking the adventurer,
The poet, the novelist, composer of song,
And though I had no map, yet I was sure
I'd come upon them if I wandered long
Among the plaques and formal portraiture,
The rows of marble headstones hundreds strong,
Eponymous mausoleums with their claim
To immortality, at least in name.

Then in the lesser alleys of the dead
Among the graven years mumbled with moss,
I felt somebody watching and turned my head,
And there a small girl stood, as at a loss,
And looked at me, as if something I'd read
Aloud was too loud, as if she might toss

Her curls and put her hands upon her hips,
But pressed instead a finger to her lips

To say, "Don't wake them," and she seemed to smile
To find herself and someone else alone
Sharing a secret for a little while,
Though I could walk away and she was stone.
I could not find among the rank and file
Among the rude democracy of bone
Any of the famous men I sought
Although I scanned the legends plot by plot.

But I found widows bent over the task
Of tending shrines, and women washing the grime
Patiently from angels who wore a mask
Where acid rain turned marble into lime.
A woman stopped me on the path to ask—
As someone asks a stranger for the time—
Where she could find the Sleeper, to lay a rose
Upon that breathless beauty's long repose.

But roaming lost amidst death's anterooms,
I did not find the exile or his bust,
Nor the swashbuckling ransacker of tombs
Who sifted stories for the golden dust
Of kings and queenly ladies at their looms,
All that was not devoured by moth or rust;
Nor the composer, nor the novelist.
The more I looked for them, the more I missed—

It was the grave of nobody I sought—
It was the purling of the ash-gray dove
In cypress boughs, and plastic flowers bought
To be the token of undying love
Some twenty years ago—they could not rot
But faded to a kind of garish mauve
Just like the fading afternoon—while I
Wandered between two dates, and earth and sky.

Pop Music

for a new parent

The music that your son will listen to
To drive you mad
Has yet to be invented. Be assured,
However, it is approaching from afar
Like the light of some Chaldean star.

On what new instruments of torture, through
What waves, lasers, wires, telepathy,
The same banalities will play
Systolic and diastolic as before,
It's hard to say—

As for the lyrics, or the lack thereof,
About love or about the lack of love,
Despite the heart's reputed amputation,
They will be as repetitive as sex
Without the imagination.

The singers will appall you, yes,
With their outlandish dress or lack of dress
Or excess hair or lack of hair, tattoos,
All aspects of their hygiene, because they remind you that he spends
Too many hours with hooligans called friends,

And while you knit another ugly sweater,
The pulsars of the brave new tunes will boom
From the hormonal miasma of his room,
Or maybe they'll just beam into his brain—
Unheard melodies are better.

Thus it has always been. Maybe that's why
The sappy retro soundtrack of your youth
Ambushes you sometimes in a café
At this almost-safe distance, and you weep, or nearly weep,
For all you knew of beauty, or of truth.

FROM *Three Poems for Psyche*

PERSEPHONE TO PSYCHE

Come sit with me here at the bar.
Another Lethe for the bride.
You're pregnant? Well, of course you are!
Make that a Virgin Suicide.

Me and my man, we tried a spell,
A pharmacopoeia of charms,
And yet . . . When I am lonesome, well,
I rock the stillborns in my arms.

This place is dead—a real dive.
We're past all twists, rewards and perils.
But what the hell. We all arrive.
Here, have some pomegranate arils.

I heard an old wives' tale above
When I was a girl with a girl's treasure.
The story went, Soul married Love
And they conceived, and called her Pleasure.

In Anhedonia we take
Our bitters with hypnotic waters.
The dawn's always about to break
But never does. We dream of daughters.

Fairy-Tale Logic

Fairy tales are full of impossible tasks:
Gather the chin hairs from a man-eating goat,
Or cross a sulfuric lake in a leaky boat,
Select the prince from a row of identical masks,
Tiptoe up to a dragon where it basks
And snatch its bone; count dust specks, mote by mote,
Or learn a phone directory by rote.
Always it's impossible what someone asks—

You have to fight magic with magic. You have to believe
That you have something impossible up your sleeve—
The language of snakes, perhaps; an invisible cloak,
An army of ants at your beck, or a lethal joke,
The will to do whatever must be done:
Marry a monster. Hand over your firstborn son.

The Catch

Something has come between us—
It will not sleep.
Every night it rises like a fish
Out of the deep.

It cries out with a human voice,
It aches to be fed.
Every night we heave it weeping
Into our bed,

With its heavy head lolled back,
Its limbs hanging down,
Like a mer-creature fetched up
From the weeds of the drowned.

Damp in the tidal dark, it whimpers,
Tossing the cover,
Separating husband from wife,
Lover from lover.

It settles in the interstice,
It spreads out its arms,
While its cool underwater face
Sharpens and warms:

This is the third thing that makes
Father and mother,
The fierce love of our fashioning
That will have no brother.

Containment

So long I have been carrying myself
Carefully, carefully, like a small child
With too much water in a real glass
Clasped in two hands, across a space as vast
As living rooms, while gazes watch the waves
That start to rile the little inland sea
(Slapping against its cliffs' transparency),
Revise and meet, double their amplitude,
Harmonizing doubt from many ifs.
Distant frowns like clouds begin to brood.
Soon there is overbrimming. Soon the child
Looks up to find a face to match the scolding,
And just as he does, the vessel he was holding
Is almost set down safely on the bookshelf.

*Accident Waiting
to Happen*

for Finn

Like the scalding cup
Of coffee you left
At the brink of the table,

I brim with potential.
I'm bright and unstable
As a just-mopped floor,

I'm a curtain near a candle,
Finger in the door,
A loose axe handle.

I'm the wrist flicked fast
With no backwards look
Blindly casting

The innocent fishhook.
I'm the toy on the stair,
The hole in the street.

I'm right in plain sight,
I'm under your feet.
I'm over your head:

I've got an edge,
And I hang by a thread.
It's almost time,

And my aim is steady.
You're falling for me,
I feel it. I'm

Ready.

Tulips

These tulips make me want to paint:
Something about the way they drop
Their petals on the tabletop
And do not wilt so much as faint,

Something about their burnt-out hearts,
Something about their pallid stems
Wearing decay like diadems,
Parading finishes like starts,

Something about the way they twist
As if to catch the last applause,
And drink the moment through long straws,
And how, tomorrow, they'll be missed.

The way they're somehow getting clearer,
The tulips make me want to *see*—
The tulips make the other me
(The backwards one who's in the mirror,

The one who can't tell left from right),
Glance now over the wrong shoulder
To watch them get a little older
And give themselves up to the light.

Alice in the Looking Glass

No longer can I just climb through—the time
Is past for going back. But you are there
Still conning books in Hebrew, right to left,
Or moving little jars on the dresser top
Like red and white pieces on a chessboard. Still
You look up curiously at me when I pass
As if you'd ask me something—maybe why
I've kept you locked inside. I'd say because
That is where I'd have reflections stay,
In surfaces, where they cannot disquiet,
Shallow, for all that they seem deep at bottom;
Though it's to you I look to set things right
(The blouse askew, hair silvering *here* and *here*)
Where everything reverses save for time.

Umbrage

Persistent little sister
Always tagging along,
Aping your every gesture
Though getting the angle wrong,

Effacing, very thin,
Born when you were born,
A kind of grim twin
Never to be torn

Away, cooler and darker,
Always underfoot,
Impermanent magic marker
That won't stay put—

On bright days she appears
A fair-weather friend,
But she's dragged you through the years,
Faithful to the end:

She's nobody's lover or wife,
She was never the pretty one;
She clings to you, though all your life
You've been standing in her sun.

Hide and Seek

My son was pretending. He said, "I am a shadow!"
He did this simply by shutting his eyes:
Inhabiting the same space as his body
While keeping all the light from coming in.
I laughed and kissed him, though it chilled me a little,
How still he stood, giving darkness his shape.

Sea Girls

for Jason

"Not gulls, *girls*." You frown, and you insist—
Between two languages, you work at words.
(R's and l's, it's hard to get them right.)
We watch the heavens' flotsam: garbage-white
Above the island dump (just out of sight),
Dirty, common, greedy—only birds.
OK, I acquiesce, too tired to banter.

Somehow they're not the same, though. See, they rise
As though we glimpsed them through a torn disguise—
Spellbound maidens, wild in flight, forsaken—
Some metamorphosis that Ovid missed,
With their pale breasts, their almost human cries.
So maybe it is I who am mistaken;
But you have changed them. You are the enchanter.

Listening to Peter and the Wolf
with Jason, Aged Three

Eyes wide open, grinning ear to ear,
Balanced between the thrill of fear and fear,
He clutches at my skirt to keep me near

And will not let me leave him by himself
In the living room where *Peter and the Wolf*
Emerges from the speakers on the shelf.

He likes Peter's jaunty swing of strings,
The reedy waddle of the duck, the wings
That flute up in the tree, but still he clings

(Even though for now it's just the cat
Picking its sneaky way through sharp and flat);
He isn't frightened of a clarinet,

And laughs at Grandfather's bluster and bassoon,
But keeps his ear out for another tune
At the shadowy edge of the wood, and coming soon.

Where is the wolf? he asks me every chance
He gets, and I explain each circumstance;
Though it's not as if he's heard it only once—

You'd think he'd know by now. *Deep in the wood,*
Or under the tree, or sent away for good
To the zoo, I say, and think he's understood,

And weary of the question and the classic,
I ask *him* where the wolf is. With grave logic
He answers me, "The wolf is in the music."

And so it is. Just then, out of the gloom
The cymbal menaces, the French horns loom.
And the music is loose. The music's in the room.

The Mother's Loathing
of Balloons

I hate you,
How the children plead
At first sight—

I want, I need,
I hate how nearly
Always I

At first say *no*,
And then comply.
(Soon, soon

They will grow bored
Clutching *your*
Umbilical cord.)

Over the moon,
Lighter-than-air,
Should you come home,

They'd cease to care—
Who tugs you through
The front door

On a leash, won't want you
Anymore
And will forget you

On the ceiling—
Admittedly,
A giddy feeling—

Later to find you
Puckered, small,
Crouching low

Against the wall.
O thin-of-skin
And fit to burst,

You break for her
Who wants you worst.
Your forebear was

The sack of the winds,
The boon that gives
And then rescinds,

Containing nothing
But the force
That blows everyone

Off course.
Once possessed,
Your one chore done,

You float like happiness
To the sun,
Untethered afternoon,

Unkind,
Marooning all
You've left behind:

Their tinfoil tears,
Their plastic cries,
Their wheedling

And moot good-byes,
You shrug them off—
You do not heed—

O loose bloom
        With no root
                No seed.

Another Bedtime Story

One day you realize it. It doesn't need to be said—
Just as you turn the page—*the end*—and close the cover—
All, all of the stories are about going to bed:

Goldilocks snug upstairs, the toothy wolf instead
Of grandmother tucked in the quilts, crooning *closer, closer*—
One day you realize it. It hardly needs to be said:

The snow-pale princess sleeps—the pillow under her head
Of rose petals or crystal—and dreams of a lost lover—
All, all of the stories are about going to bed;

Even the one about witches and ovens and gingerbread
In the dark heart of Europe—can children save each other?—
You start to doubt it a little. It doesn't need to be said,

But I'll say it, because it's embedded in everything I've read,
The tales that start with *once* and end with *ever after*,
All, all of the stories are about going to bed,

About coming to terms with the night, alleviating the dread
Of laying the body down, of lying under a cover.
That's why our children resist it so. That's why it mustn't be said:
All, all of the stories are about going to bed.

OLIVES

Is love
so evil?
Is Eve? Lo,
love vies,
evolves. I
lose selves,
sylphs of
loose Levi's,
sieve oil of
vile sloe.
Love sighs,
slives. O
veils of
voile, so
sly, so suave.
O lives,
soil sleeves,
I love so
I solve.

From

LIKE

(2018)

After a Greek Proverb

Ουδέν μονιμότερον του προσωρινού

We're here for the time being, I answer to the query—
Just for a couple of years, we said, a dozen years back.
Nothing is more permanent than the temporary.

We dine sitting on folding chairs—they were cheap but cheery.
We've taped the broken windowpane. TV's still out of whack.
We're here for the time being, I answer to the query.

When we crossed the water, we only brought what we could carry,
But there are always boxes that you never do unpack.
Nothing is more permanent than the temporary.

Sometimes when I'm feeling weepy, you propose a theory:
Nostalgia and tear gas have the same acrid smack.
We're here for the time being, I answer to the query—

We stash bones in the closet when we don't have time to bury,
Stuff receipts in envelopes, file papers in a stack.
Nothing is more permanent than the temporary.

Twelve years now and we're still eating off the ordinary:
We left our wedding china behind, afraid that it might crack.
We're here for the time being, we answer to the query,
But nothing is more permanent than the temporary.

Ajar

The washing-machine door broke.   We hand-washed for a week.
Left in the tub to soak,   the angers began to reek,
And sometimes when we spoke,   you said we shouldn't speak.

Pandora was a bride—   the gods gave her a jar
But said don't look inside.   You know how stories are—
The can of worms denied?   It's never been so far.

Whatever the gods forbid,   it's sure someone will do,
And so Pandora did,   and made the worst come true,
She peeked under the lid,   and out all trouble flew:

Sickness, war, and pain,   nerves frayed like fretted rope,
Every mortal bane   with which Mankind must cope—
The only thing to remain,   lodged in the mouth, was Hope.

Or so the tale asserts—   and who am I to deny it?—
Yes, out like black-winged birds,   the woes flew and ran riot,
But I say that the woes were words,   and the only thing left was quiet.

Alice, Bewildered

Deep in the wood where things escape their names,
Her childish arm draped round the fawn's soft neck
(Her diffidence, its skittishness in check,
Merged in the anonymity that tames),
She knits her brow, but nothing now reclaims
The syllables that meant herself. Ah well,
She need not answer to the grown-up beck
And call, the rote-learned lessons, scolds and blames
Of girlhood, sentences to parse and gloss;
She's un-twinned from the likeness in the glass.
Yet in the dark ellipsis she can tell,
She's certain, that her name begins with "L"—
Liza, Lacie? Alias, alas,
A lass alike alone and at a loss.

Art Monster

My mother fell for beauty,
Although it was another species,
Ox-eyed, dew-lapped, groomed for sacrifice.

She had to devise another self
To put her self in—something inhuman
Or beauty could not possess her—

(O daedal mechanics!)
She grew huge with hybridity,
Rumor-ripened. I was born

To be amazed.
She fascinated me with cat's cradles,
Spun threads out of my hirsute

Hair shirt. I was fed
On raw youths and maidens,
When all I wanted was the cud of clover.

I was named after my step-
Father, dispenser of judgment,
No one called me my mother's son.

Minotaur, they said, O Minotaur,
You are unnatural, grotesque.
A hero will come to slay you, a hero

Who jilts princesses on desert islands.
It is heroic to slay, to break a heart,
To solve the archaic puzzle in the basement,

De-monster the darkness.
I await this patiently, as I bow to the yoke
Of making, scratching this earliest of inscriptions

On a potsherd, down here in the midden,
Writing left to right, then right
To left, as a broken beast furrows a field.

Cast Irony

Who scrubbed this iron skillet
In water, with surfactant soap,
Meant to cleanse, not kill it,

But since its black and lustrous skin
Despoiled of its enrobing oils,
Dulled, lets water in,

Now it is vulnerable and porous
As a hero stripped of his arms
Before a scornful chorus.

It lacks
Internal consistency
As ancient oral epics

Where a Bronze Age warrior might appeal
To a boar's-tusk-helmet-wearing foe
Who has an anachronistic heart of steel,

Will of iron—from which metals
No one has yet forged a weapon,
Much less pans or kettles

(Though there must have been between
Two eras, awkward overlap
Enacted in the kitchen

When mother-in-law and daughter
Wrangled over the newfangled,
Over oil and water

In proverbial mistrust,
Brazen youth subject to iron age
As iron is to rust).

There can be no reasoning
With sarcastic oxygen,
Only a re-seasoning

Can give the vessel's life new lease:
Scour off the scab the color of dried blood,
Apply some elbow grease

To make it fast;
Anoint it, put it once more in the fire
Where everything is cast.

Colony Collapse Disorder

(Iliad, 2.87–2.90)

Just as a swarm pours from a hollow rock
In one long beeline for the wild thyme,
Alighting in clusters on this purple and that,
But is stricken with a mass amnesia
That disorients the compass of the sun,
And they forget the steps to traditional dances,
And each helicopters into a different dimness
Taking their saddlebags of sweetness with them,
And the hive goes dark, the queen is left to starve,
And the drones humbug the whimper of the world,
And the palace falls to ruins, broken into
By vandals who would loot the golden stores
Left in the brittle wax hexameters,
Just so . . .

Denouement

Woolgathering afternoon:
All I've accomplished, all,
Is to untangle a wine-dark skein
And coil it into a ball.

I did not knit a swatch
For gauge—or cast a stitch—
Or pick a plausible pattern out,
I just unworked one hitch

After another, and went
Brailling along the maze,
Over, under, twist and turn,
To where the ending frays.

It's always best to leave
No glitches in the plot;
Sailors tell you that the yarn
Is weakest at the knot.

Open, do not tug
The little nooses closed,
Tease the cat from her cradle, lead
The minotaur by the nose

Out of the labyrinth
Through which all heroes travel,
And where the waiting wife will learn
To ravel's to unravel.

Out of the complicated,
Roll the smooth, round One,
So when it drops out of your lap
It brightly comes undone,

Leaping over the floor
Like swift ships outward-bound,
Unfurling the catastrophe
That aches to be rewound.

Dyeing the Easter Eggs

Dyeing the Easter eggs, the children talk
Of dying. Resurrection's in the air
Like the whiff of vinegar. These eggs won't hatch,
My daughter says, since they are cooked and dead,
A hard-boiled batch.

I am the children's blonde American mother,
Who thinks that Easter eggs should be pastel—
But they have icon eyes, and they are Greek.
And eggs should be, they've learned at school this week,
Blood red.

We compromise, and some are yellow, or blue,
Or red and blue, assorted purples, mauves,
But most are crimson, a hematic hue,
Rubbed to a sheen with chrism of olive oil;
They will not spoil,

As Christian death is a preservative,
As Jesus trampled death and harrowed Hell.
The kids' palms are incarnadine and violet,
A mess! Go wash your hands! They wash their hands,
Punctilious as Pontius Pilate.

Empathy

My love, I'm grateful tonight
Our listing bed isn't a raft
Precariously adrift
As we dodge the coast guard light,

And clasp hold of a girl and a boy.
I'm glad we didn't wake
Our kids in the thin hours, to take
Not a thing, not a favorite toy,

And didn't hand over our cash
To one of the smuggling rackets,
That we didn't buy cheap life jackets
No better than bright orange trash

And less buoyant. I'm glad that the dark
Above us is not deeply twinned
Beneath us, and moiled with wind,
And we don't scan the sky for a mark,

Any mark, that demarcates a shore
As the dinghy starts taking on water.
I'm glad that our six-year-old daughter,
Who can't swim, is a foot off the floor

In the bottom bunk, and our son
With his broken arm's high and dry,
That the ceiling is not seeping sky,
With our journey but hardly begun.

Empathy isn't generous,
It's selfish. It's not being nice
To say I would pay any price
Not to be those who'd die to be us.

Epic Simile

for Rachel Hadas

Right shoulder aching with daylong butchery,
Left shoulder numb with dints clanged on the shield,
The hero is fouled with blood, his own and others',
First slick, then sticky, then caked, starting to mat
His beard—the armor deadweight all around him;
His teeth grit and rattle with every jolt
Of bronze-rimmed wheels behind the shit-flecked horses.
But when he glimpses the mountains, the distant snow,
A blankness swoons upon him, and he hears
Nothing but the white vowels of the wind
Brushing through stands of spears like conifers
While a banner slips its staff and hangs in the blue
Like a kestrel or a contrail. The hero's death,
The prize, elusive quarry of his life,
Stands stock-still in her cloven tracks in snow
And turns, one ear tuned to the creek's far bank,
One dished towards him. Her unstartled gaze
Beads on him like a sniper's sights, until
At the clean report of a cracking poplar branch,
She leaps away like luck, over rapid water,
And snowfall scrims the scene like a mist of tears,
Like a migraine, like sweat or blood streaming into your eyes.

First Miracle

Her body like a pomegranate torn
Wide open, somehow bears what must be born,

The irony where a stranger small enough
To bed down in the ox-tongue-polished trough

Erupts into the world and breaks the spell
Of the ancient, numbered hours with his yell.

Now her breasts ache and weep and soak her shirt
Whenever she hears his hunger or his hurt;

She can't change water into wine; instead
She fashions sweet milk out of her own blood.

For Atalanta

Your name is long and difficult, I know.
So many people whom we didn't ask
Have told us so
And taken us to task.
You too perhaps will wonder as you grow

And blame us with the venom of thirteen
For ruining your life,
Using our own love against us, keen
As a double-bladed knife.
Already I can picture the whole scene.

How will we answer you?
Yes, you were in a hurry to arrive
As if it were a race to be alive.
We weighed the syllables, and they rang true,
And we were hoping too

You'd come to like the stories
Of princesses who weren't set on shelves
Like china figurines. Not allegories,
But girls whose glories
Included rescuing themselves,

Slaying their own monsters, running free
But not running away. It might be rough

Singled out for singularity.
Tough.
Beauty will be of some help. You'll see.

But it is not enough
To be nimble, brave, or fleet.
O apple of my eye, the world will drop
Many gilded baubles at your feet
To break your stride: don't look down, don't stoop

To scoop them up, don't stop.

Glitter

All that will remain after an apocalypse is glitter.
—British *Vogue*

You have a daughter now. It's everywhere,
And often in the company of glue.
You can't get rid of it. It's in her hair:
A wink of pink, a glint of silver-blue.
It's catching, like the chicken pox, or lice.
It travels, like a planetary scar.
Sometimes it's on your face, or you look twice
And glimpse, there on your arm, a single star.
You know it by a hand's brushing your neck—
You blush—it's not desire, not anymore—
Just someone's urge to flick away the fleck
Of borrowed glamour from your collarbone—
The broken mirror Time will not restore,
The way your daughter marks you as her own.

Half of an Epic Simile
Not Found in Hesiod

As at the winter solstice, when a faded blonde
On the brink of middle age goes to the salon
To brighten up her outlook and her spirits
(Warm water on her scalp, the rich shampoo
That breathes of almond blossoms), to submit
To another's expert disinterested caresses,
While outside the plate-glass window, people push
Against the dwindling year, and lean into
The wind, their foreheads pinched with doubt and debt,
And it's afternoon, but night comes chattering down
Like the shutters of a shop in a recession,
And all she asks for is a color adjustment,
For rays of honey to eclipse the grey,
And for the light to lengthen just a little.

The Last Carousel

The horses have seen better days go by
With the one eye that peers
Out on the orbiting world. The other eye

Has always looked inward, to where the moving parts
Are hidden by a column of gilt-edged tarnished mirrors.
Why are we pierced through our hearts

By their poles of polished brass?
Mismatched orphans, some antique,
Carved of solid wood, some factory-molded fiberglass,

They course counterclockwise, round and round,
While Time holds them at arm's length.
Their feet are shod but never touch the ground.

They've known the shake of reins bidding them race,
The heels that drum their flanks
Urging them faster and faster in one place,

The laughter and the outside voices calling,
The tinned music stuttering in its rut,
The last seasick tide rising or falling.

Their gallop is a wave that seizes.
In their rhythmic progression, they are cousin to the horses
On stolen, marble friezes,

In bas-relief, in some far-off museum,
That once were prinked with paint.
But now that I see them

Waiting patiently beneath the hive of garish light,
As one giddy generation mounts,
And another sulks into the night—

One last go, it isn't fair!—
I am moved by the pivot of their stillness,
By their ragged comet tails of genuine horsehair.

Like, the Sestina

with a nod to Jonah Winter

Now we're all "friends," there is no love but Like,
A semi-demi-goddess, something like
A reality-TV-star look-alike,
Named Simile or Me Two. So we like
In order to be liked. It isn't like
There's Love or Hate now. Even plain "dislike"

Is frowned on: there's no button for it. Like
Is something you can quantify: each "like"
You gather's almost something money-like,
Token of virtual support. "Please like
This page to stamp out hunger." And you'd like
To end hunger and climate change alike,

But it's unlikely Like does diddly. Like
Just twiddles its unopposing thumbs-ups, like-
Wise props up scarecrow silences. "I'm like,
So OVER him," I overhear. "But, like,
He doesn't get it. Like, you know? He's like
It's all OK. Like I don't even LIKE

Him anymore. Whatever. I'm all like . . ."
Take "like" out of our chat, we'd all alike
Flounder, agape, gesticulating like

A foreign film sans subtitles, fall like
Dumb phones to mooted desuetude. Unlike
With other crutches, um, when we use "like,"

We're not just buying time on credit: Like
Displaces other words; crowds, cuckoo-like,
Endangered hatchlings from the nest. (Click "like"
If you're against extinction!) Like is like
Invasive zebra mussels, or it's like
Those nutria things, or kudzu, or belike

Redundant fast-food franchises, each like
(More like) the next. Those poets who dislike
Inversions, archaisms, who just like
Plain English as she's spoke—why isn't "like"
Their (literally) every other word? I'd like
Us just to admit that's what real speech is like.

But as you like, my friend. Yes, we're alike
How we pronounce, say, "lichen," and dislike
Cancer and war. So like this page. Click *Like*.

Lost and Found

I.

I crawled all morning on my hands and knees
Searching for what was lost—beneath a chair,
Behind the out-of-tune piano. *Please*,
I prayed to Entropy, let it be there—
Some vital Lego brick or puzzle piece
(A child bereft is hiccoughing despair),
A ball, a doll's leg popped out of its socket,
Or treasures fallen through a holey pocket.

II.

Amazing what webbed shadows can conceal—
A three-wheeled Matchbox car, or half a brace
Of socks or shoes. Oblivion will steal
Promiscuously—lost without a trace,
Microscopic bits of Playmobil,
The backup set of house keys. You misplace
Your temper and your wits, till you exhaust
All patience with the hours it has cost.

III.

I thought too of that parable, the other—
Not the one men preach of the lost sheep,
The lesser-known one, on the housewife's bother
Over a missing coin: how she must sweep
The house to find it. No doubt, *she* was a mother,
I think, and laugh, and then I want to weep:
The hours drained as women rearrange
The furniture in search of small, lost change.

IV.

"Tidy up your room," I told my son,
"That way, it's easier to look." (It's true.)
He made an effort, a halfhearted one
Abandoned after just a block or two.
"It isn't fair," he said, "it isn't fun,
I never do what *I* would like to do,
But you, you always do *just what you want.*"
Which plucked a string, as though a cosmic taunt.

V.

I paused. "Is *that* what you think, then," I said.
(Sometimes he seemed less seven-year-old boy
Than teenager.) "That making you go to bed
Or washing dishes is something I *enjoy*,
And that I've nothing better to do instead
Of hunting for a crappy plastic toy?"
Raised voices, tears, apologies all round,
And yet the crucial piece was never found.

VI.

That night I was still seeking in my dreams,
Still groping after fragments and the maimed,
Just as in dreams a seamstress stitches seams,
Or politician spins truth unashamed,
Or, loping through remembered fields and streams,
The hound pursues the scent that can't be named,
Her paws a-twitch, though heavily she lies,
And dogsbody the body does not rise,

VII.

Or as a poet stalks a skittish rhyme
Behind her lidded eyes, beneath the mask
Of sleep—because the mind has no free time
But keeps at night to its diurnal task
And pushes the stone as high as it can climb
Before it trochees down again. Don't ask
The mind to rest, though someday it must cease;
In life, only the flesh has any peace.

VIII.

It seemed I searched, though, in a dusty place
Beneath a black sky thrilled with stars, ground strewn
With stones whose blotting shade seemed to erase
The land's gleam (like a tarnished silver spoon);
A figure neared, with adumbrated face,
Who said, "This is the valley on the moon
Where everything misplaced on earth accrues,
And here all things are gathered that you lose."

IX.

The moon? Yet I did not dispute the claim.
She seemed familiar—hard to tell among
Such alien surroundings. All the same,
A word seemed out of reach, tip of my tongue,
Close-clustered consonants and vowels, a name.
Beneath her hood I glimpsed a face not young
But elegant, refined as it grew older.
My name she knew, although I hadn't told her.

X.

Now that my eyes had focused in the dark
I saw that what seemed mountains, ridges, hills
All hemmed around us, flinging down their stark
Chill silhouettes, were overflowing landfills,
Huge heaps of congeries. And I could mark
The mounds of keys or orphaned socks, dropped pills
(Those were the things that I could recognize),
Like bombed-out cities black against the skies.

XI.

Somehow it brought to mind the vestibule
Jumbled with hats, umbrellas, backpacks, totes,
Scarves, gym shoes, that they keep at my son's school
Behind the lunchroom: bins of winter coats,
Hairbands, sunglasses stacked up on a stool—
Each thing spoke volumes or quipped anecdotes—
Lorn, makeless gloves; lunch boxes starting to mottle.
(I'd come to seek an AWOL water bottle.)

XII.

"Look there," she said, and gestured to the keys,
"Those are the halls to which we can't return—
The rooms where we once sat on others' knees,
Grandparents' houses, loving, spare, and stern,
Tree houses where we whispered to the trees
Gauche secrets, virgin bedrooms where we'd burn,
Love's first apartments. As we shut each door,
It locks: we cannot enter anymore."

XIII.

There was a mound that loomed above our heads,
A skein of dusty strands large as a barn.
"Are these," I asked, "the sum of hair one sheds
In life, or all the rips one has to darn?"
She laughed and said, "Those are the frayed, lost threads
Of conversations, arguments, the yarn
Of thought and logic's clews we'd thought we'd spun
Only to find they'd somehow come undone."

XIV.

Then there was sunk, among the hills, a bowl,
A wide, shallow depression, in which "O"s
Or ciphers gathered, thin, and black as coal,
Like washers of black iron. I asked, "And those?"
"They mark our absences—it's through the hole
Of lapsed attention that the moment goes."
I thought of those assemblies with repentance
Where I had mocked the prizes of attendance.

xv.

"And that?" I pointed to a pyramid
Of papers, ever threatening to tumble.
It shifted—sheaves of pages suddenly slid
Then seemed to settle. I stepped back from the jumble,
Thinking we might be buried there amid
An avalanche of foolscap. A hushed rumble
Shuffled its menace. I whispered, "Then are those
The poems lost, or pages of sure prose—

xvi.

"Maybe even something that would sell
(A book about a young aspiring warlock?)—
That disappeared when something broke the spell,
When toddler learned to work the study door-lock,
Or telephone brayed bad news—or the front bell
Portended importunity from Porlock?"
"The poems," she said, "that perish at the brink
Of being, aren't so many as you think,

XVII.

"Nor yet so great. No, no, these are the letters
We meant to write and didn't—all the unsaid
Begrudged congratulations to our betters,
Condolences we owed the lately dead,
Love notes unsent—in love, we all are debtors—
Gratitude to teachers who penned in red
Corrections to our ignorant defenses,
Apologies kept close like confidences."

XVIII.

A vague, headachy cloud among the towers
Rose, as heaps of grey down from black swans.
"Those are," she said, "Insomnia's desperate hours,
Lost sleep: countdown of clocks, the impotent yawns;
The teething cries, sweet drowsiness that sours,
The night feedings that soldier into dawns."
I watched as creatures, etiolated, pale,
Weighed bales of feathers in a brazen scale.

XIX.

What were the creatures doing? She explained,
"For every hour that we lose of sleep,
Another hour of wakefulness is gained;
There is a tally that we have to keep."
"Unbearable minutes!" She saw that I was pained.
"Perhaps," she said, "but sometimes in the deep
Of night, reflections come we cannot parse—
To *consider* means to contemplate the stars."

XX.

Skittering round us, skirls of silver sand
Would swarm and arch into a ridge or dune,
And then disperse, as if an unseen hand
Swept them away (there was no wind), then soon
Accumulate elsewhere, a sarabande
Of form and entropy, a restive swoon
Of particles, forever in a welter,
Like starling murmurations seeking shelter.

XXI.

"The sands of Time." (I didn't have to speak;
She answered straightaway with some disdain.)
"With scything hands you hasten through the week
Clockwise, while widdershins, the fair hours drain.
Haste," she declared, "is Violence, in Greek."
Then she bore on in silence once again.
"Why won't they rest?" I asked in puzzlement.
"Minutes are not lost," she said, "but spent."

XXII.

Nearby, a glint of vitreous splinters, foiled
With silver, bristled in a jagged mass.
"This is a woman's loveliness that's spoiled
With age," she said, "and tears, and days that pass—
Her raiment that is creased, thread-worn, and soiled.
Here, seek that vanished beauty in this glass."
And gave me a reflection where I sought her—
Nothing at first—but then I saw my daughter—

XXIII.

Eyes brown, not blue; the hair, not straight, but curled.
"Not truly lost," she laughed, at my surprise.
"Some things fetch up on the bright shores of the world
Once more, under a slightly different guise;
Meanwhile, they are not lost, but somehow furled
Back in the heart of things from which they rise."
And saying this, she turned, and did not wait,
But something nearby made me hesitate,

XXIV.

I couldn't make it out at first: a pile
Of bone chips, ivory splinters? Like a sleuth,
I sneaked a handful, following the while,
But stopped short when I realized the truth,
And let them fall, and dropped my neutral smile:
Each keen point was a tiny human tooth.
I looked back over my shoulder for a glimpse
And gasped to see a thousand small, grey imps

XXV.

Go scampering up the hill, with wrinkled wings
Leathern like bats, with backs hunched up to carry,
Slung on their shoulders, sacks bulged with grim things—
More teeth, I thought—remains you ought to bury.
My guide observed me watch their scurryings.
"But don't you recognize a real tooth fairy?
Each baby tooth, deciduous but bright,
Stands for a childhood rooted in delight,

XXVI.

"But those that come here stained, starting to rot,
Are childhoods that are eaten up with sorrow,
Eroded by the acids of their lot,
And others' sins they are compelled to borrow."
"So many!" I exclaimed, as fairies brought
More chatterings of teeth. "Yes, and tomorrow,
It never stops. Each childhood is outgrown
By sharper permanence. Even your own"

XXVII.

(Children, she meant) "cannot stay as they are.
Already, your son's childhood is consigned"—
She held up six fine milk teeth in a jar—
"Already he is leaving it behind,
Striding forth as light strides from a star;
And though the star blow out, inert and blind,
The light strides on, and reaches other eyes
That in some distant time scan these same skies."

XXVIII.

At last our path came to a spring whose gleam
Provoked my thirst. Two cups of battered zinc
Hung from a pair of hooks there: one had "Dream"
Inscribed upon it; on the other, "Think."
But when I dipped each cup's lip to the stream,
Immediately it began to sink.
When both had vanished, she said, "Do not wet
Your lips here with the waters of Forget."

XXIX.

Not water, though, I knew as I drew near it—
It was a liquid, true, but more like gin
Though smelling of aniseed—some cold, clear spirit
Water turns cloudy. "Many are taken in,
Some poets seek it, thinking that they fear it,
The reflectionless fountain of Oblivion.
By sex, by pills, by leap of doubt, by gas,
Or at the bottom of a tilting glass.

XXX.

"But you, you must remember, and return,"
Now I saw clearly skin of alabaster,
Her moon-washed hair, a gaze one could discern
As gunmetal grey—and then at last I asked her,
"Who are you? Are you She who used to burn
With sweetbitter eros? Or She who learned to master
The art of losing? She who did dying well,
Beekeeper's waspish daughter? Amherst's belle?"

XXXI.

"Don't you know? But everyone who loses
Has prayed and laid an offering at my shrine—
Though each who knows me calls me as she chooses,
My name's Mnemosyne; I am divine.
I am," she said, "the Mother of the Muses—
Imagine, you have two, but I have nine!
More even than that—for all the arts that be,
Sciences too, are born of Memory."

XXXII.

It made me smile, to think of her at her loom,
A gaggle of teenaged daughters at her feet:
No-nonsense Clio, Melpomene gothed in gloom,
Graceful Euterpe, Terpsichore, who won't eat,
Polyhymnia, with incense for perfume,
Thalia, laughing, Urania taking a seat
At the telescope, Erato fine-tuning her fiddle,
Calliope starting her story in the middle.

XXXIII.

She led the way now through a garden of musks
From dark, fanged flowers—incarnadine, maroon.
We came upon two gates: one made of tusks
Of prehistoric elephants, one hewn
From massive, savage horns. All round, the husks
And bones of great extinctions had been strewn.
"Here we must pass," she said, "but not together.
You pass through one; I shall go through the other."

XXXIV.

Then something began to happen. I felt her arm
On mine, we seemed to travel, standing still,
I saw a light. Had someone come to harm?
I heard a distant siren, pulsing, shrill—
But then I recognized the old alarm
Harping on its monitory trill—
It's Dawn again, come with her golden rule
Like a shepherd's crook, to harry us to school.

XXXV.

There are lunches to make, I thought, and tried to find
Some paperwork from last week I'd mislaid
(Due back, no doubt, today, dated and signed),
Instead, unearthed a bill we hadn't paid,
Located shoes, a scarf, a change of mind:
I tried to put aside mistakes I'd made,
To live in the sublunary, the swift,
Deep present, through which falling bodies sift.

XXXVI.

I saw the aorist moment as it went—
The light on my children's hair, my face in the glass
Neither old nor young; but bare, intelligent.
I was a sieve—I felt the moment pass
Right through me, currency as it was spent,
That bright, loose change, like falling leaves, that mass
Of decadent gold leaf, now turning brown—
I could not keep it; I could write it down.

Memorial (Mnemosyno)

You'd lost your father's grave.
We wandered row by row and plot by plot.
And it was hot
Under stiff cypress shade, the stillness drowned
By a lone insect's corrugated sound.

You went on ahead
To inquire of the bureaucracy of the dead.
Overdressed, uncomfortable as guilt,
We stood around, not knowing how to behave.
The kids began to wilt,

And there was nowhere to sit that wasn't a tomb.
Each grave was kitted out
With a dustpan and a little broom
To tidy the garden beds of the bereft,
And here and there hung plastic watering cans

Chained to headstones and trees—without a doubt,
Even in this place, there was a problem with theft.
Then you came back
With the coordinates, and snagged a priest
Glistening in polyester black,

Who, at the grave, now found,
Spoke of the rest and rising of the dead
As if they were so many loaves of bread
Tucked in their oblong pans
In a kitchen gold with sunlight, rich with yeast.

Momentary

I never glimpse her but she goes
Who had been basking in the sun,
Her links of chain mail one by one
Aglint with pewter, bronze, and rose.

I never see her lying coiled
Atop the garden step, or under
A dark leaf, unless I blunder
And by some motion she is foiled.

Too late I notice as she passes
Zither of chromatic scale—
I only ever see her tail
Quicksilver into tall grasses.

I know her only by her flowing,
By her glamour disappearing
Into shadow as I'm nearing—
I only recognize her going.

Pencil

Once, you loved permanence,
Indelible. You'd sink
Your thoughts in a black well,
And called the error, ink.

And then you crossed it out;
You cancelled as you went.
But you craved permanence,
And honored the intent.

Perfection was a blot
That could not be undone.
You honored what was not,
And it was legion.

And you were sure, so sure,
But now you cannot *stay* sure.
You turn the point around
And honor the erasure.

Rubber stubs the page,
The heart, a stiletto of lead,
And all that was black and white
Is in-between instead.

All scratch, all sketch, all note,
All tentative, all tensile
Line that is not broken,
But pauses with the pencil,

And all choice, multiple,
The quiz that gives no quarter,
And Time the other implement
That sharpens and grows shorter.

Placebo

No can do. I am
doctor not of medicine,
but Latinity.

I am the future,
singular, indicative.
The first person. What

do you take me for?
If is a real condition.
If I'm a pill, then

you are double blind.
What you don't know can't hurt you.
Spoonful of sugar,

it's all in your head,
this dendritic alchemy
of pain. Nothing works.

FROM **Refugee Fugue**

Appendix A: Useful Phrases in
Arabic, Farsi/Dari, and Greek
(*found poem, from the* Guide to Volunteering
in Athens, *as updated for March 17, 2016*)

Welcome to Greece!
Thank God for your safe arrival (greeting after trip)
Hello
Good morning
Good evening
Good night
Thank you
You're welcome
Please
I don't understand
I don't speak Arabic / Farsi
Slowly
Come here
You're safe
Are you wet / cold?
Yes / No
My name is . . .
What is your name?
He / She / It is
We / They are
God is with the patient (will make people laugh)

Give yourself a break (comforting words)

Free (no charge)

Refugee

Volunteer

Foreigner

Friend

I am hungry

Thirsty

Food

Water

Does it hurt?

Sick

Pregnant

Mother / Father

Brother / Sister

Child

Family

What country is your family from?

Pharmacy

Medicine

Hospital

Doctor

Tent

Sorry, it has run out

We do not have it now

New shoes only if yours are broken

Wait here, please

I will return soon

Follow me / Come with me

Come back in . . .
5 / 15 / 45 minutes
One hour
Quarter / Half hour / Half day
Today / Tomorrow / Yesterday
How many people?
Sorry
Stay calm
One line, please

Next person

The Rosehead Nail

Blacksmithing demonstration, Monteagle, Tennessee

"But can you forge a nail?" the pale boy asks,
And the blacksmith shoves a length of iron rod
Deep in the coal fire cherished by the bellows
Until it glows volcanic. He was a god
Before anachronism, before the tasks
That had been craft were jobbed out to machine.
By dint of hammer-song he makes his keen,
Raw point, and crowns utility with rose:
Quincunx of facets petaling its head.
The breeze-made-visible sidewinds. The boy's
Blonde mother shifts and coughs. *Once Work was wed
To Loveliness*—sweat-faced, swarthy from soot, he
Reminds us with the old saw he employs
(And doesn't miss a beat): "Smoke follows beauty."

Scissors

Are singular, and plural, un-
Canny: *one plus one is one*;

Even in solitude, a pair,
Cheek to cheek, or on a tear,

Knives at cross-purposes, bereaving
Cleavers to each other cleaving:

Open, shut; give and take,
All dichotomy in their wake.

What starts with sighs, concludes in "or"s:
His or hers; mine or yours:

Divvy up. Slice clean, slice deep,
In pinked jags, or one swift sweep,

The crisp sheet where they met and married,
The paper where the blades are buried.

Sea Urchins

The sea urchins star
the seafloor like sunken mines
from a rust-smirched war

filmed in black and white.
Or if they are stars they are
negatives of light,

their blind beams brittle
purple needles with no eyes:
not even spittle

and a squint will thread
the sea's indigo ribbons.
We float overhead

like angels, or whales,
with our soft underbellies
just beyond their pales,

their dirks and rankles.
Nothing is bare as bare feet,
naked as ankles.

They whisker their risks
in the fine print of footnotes'
irksome asterisks.

Their extraneous
complaints are lodged with dark dots,
subcutaneous

ellipses . . . seizers
seldom extract even with
olive oil, tweezers.

Sun-bleached, they unclench
their sharps, doom scalps their hackles,
unbuttons their stench.

Their shells are embossed
and beautiful calculus,
studded turbans, tossed

among drummed pebbles
and plastic flotsam—so smooth,
so fragile, baubles

like mermaid doubloons,
these rose-, mauve-, pistachio-
tinted macaroons.

Selvage

(from self + edge, *the firmly woven edge*
of a fabric that resists unravelling)

(Odyssey, 22.468–473)

Who knew her son had salvaged so many hates?
Their feet twitched a little, like thrushes caught
In a fowler's net. The simile had the tang
Of remorse. No, surely the idea was his
To hoist them up like flags in their long skirts,
Modest now, the sluts, the dirty flirts,
Tongueless belles, spinsters of their own doom.
While they twitched, a flutter of pity. But as it is
She finds them tidy and domesticated,
Dull plumaged with death, now that they hang,
As if in the spotlit vitrine of a future museum,
From the warp like a dozen ancient loom weights.

Shattered

Another smashed glass,
wrong end of a gauche gesture
towards a cliff—compass-

rose of mis-direc-
tions, scattered to the twelve winds,
the wine-dark sea wreck.

Wholeness won't stay put.
Why these sweeping conclusions?
Always you're barefoot,

nude-soled in a room
fanged with recriminations,
leaning on a broom.

How can you know what's
missing, unless you puzzle
all the shards? What cuts

is what's overlooked,
the sliver of the unseen,
faceted, edged, hooked,

unremarked atom
of remorse broadcast across
lame linoleum.

Archaeologist
of the just-made mistake, sift
smithereens of schist

for the unhidden
right-in-plain-sight needling
mote in the midden.

Fragments, say your feet,
make the shivered, shimmering
brokenness complete.

Shoulda, Woulda, Coulda

The mood made him tense—
How she sharpened conditional futures
On strops of might-have-beens,
The butchered present in sutures.

He cursed in the fricative,
The way she could not act.
Or live in the indicative,
Only contrary to fact.

Tomorrow should have been vast,
Bud-packed, grenade-gravid,
Not just a die miscast.

It made him sad, it made him livid:
How she construed from the imperfect past
A future less vivid.

Silence

Silence has its own notation: dark
Jottings of duration, but not pitch,
A long black box, or little feathered hitch
Like a new Greek letter or diacritical mark.
Silence is a function of Time, the lark
In flight but not in song. A nothing which
Keeps secrets or confesses. Pregnant, rich,
Or awkward, cold, the pause that makes us hark,
The space before or after: it's the room
In which melody moves, the medium
Through which thought travels, it is golden, best,
Welcome relief to talk-worn tedium.
Before the word itself, it was the womb.
It has a measure. Music calls it rest.

FROM **Similes, Suitors**

2. Book Omega

The suitors' skittish shades began to squeak
Like the scritch of a toxic-fumed permanent marker
Scratching off the names of those who are absent,
Or as when deep in a cave, a small brown bat
Plummets to the guano-spackled basement
Jagged with assorted speleothems
And the colony of bats is all a-twitter,
A roost that's been afflicted with the fungus
That causes the contagious white-nose syndrome
Which strikes during hibernation, rousing the bats
From torpor early, stirring them to starve,
And they gibber like dementia from the cave's mouth
Into the starless, cold night of extinction,
Taking with them a white night-blooming flower
Dependent on chiropterophily,
Just so the suitors pipistrelled and bleeped,
Trailing the lord of florists, with his wand
And Nike sandals, He who delivers a species
Like a bouquet of spiky asphodel,
Appalled with pollen, to the halls of Hell.

The Stain

Remembers
Your embarrassment,
Wine or blood,
Sweat or oil,

When the ink leaked
Your intent
Because you thought
No truth could soil,

Or when you let
The secret slip,
Or when you dropped
The leaden hint,

Or when between
The cup and lip,
The Beaujolais
Pled innocent,

Or when the rumor's
Fleet was launched,
Or when the sheets
Waged their surrender,

But the breach
Could not be staunched
And no apology
Would tender;

When over-served,
You misconstrued
And blurbed your heartsick
On your sleeve,

When everything
Became imbued
With sadness, yet
You couldn't grieve.

Inalienable
As DNA,
Self-evident
As fingerprints,

It will not out
Although you spray
And presoak in the sink
And rinse:

What they suspect
The stain will know,
The stain records
What you forget.

If you wear it,
It will show;
If you wash it,
It will set.

Sunset, Wings

Crows descry the sky,
desecrate the cyanic,
scrying and crying.

Swallows, I swear, not
swifts; but swift—swoop, swivel—whose
scissored silhouettes,

belated, become
a quibble of pipistrelles,
tippling acrobats.

Who haunts the hill? Lo,
one-note woe: oh well, twilight
throws in the towel.

Swallows

Every year the swallows come
And put their homestead in repair,
And raise another brood, and skim
And boomerang through summer air,
And reap mosquitoes from the hum
Of holidays. A handsome pair,
One on the nest, one on the wire,
Cheat-cheat-cheat, the two conspire

To murder half the insect race,
And feed them squirming to their chicks.
They work and fret at such a pace,
And natter in between, with clicks
And churrs, they lift the raftered place
(Seaside taverna) with their tricks
Of cursive loops and Morse-code call,
Both analog and digital.

They seem to us so coupled, married,
So flustered with their needful young,
So busy housekeeping, so harried,
It's hard to picture them among
The origins of myth—a buried
Secret, rape, a cut-out tongue,
Two sisters wronged, where there's no right,
Till transformation fledges flight.

But Ovid swapped them in the tale,
So that the sister who was forced
Becomes instead the nightingale,
Who sings as though her heart would burst.
It's Ovid's stories that prevail.
And thus the swallow is divorced
Twice from her voice, her tuneless chatter,
And no one asks her what's the matter.

These swallows, though, don't have the knack
For sorrow—or we'd not have guessed—
Though smartly dressed in tailored black,
Spend no time mourning, do not rest,
One scissors forth, one zigzags back,
They take turns settled on the nest
Or waiting on a perch nearby
To zero in on wasp or fly.

They have no time for tragic song,
As dusk distills, they dart and flicker,
The days are long, but not as long
As yesterday. The night comes quicker,
And soon the season will be wrong.
Knackered, cross, they bitch and bicker,
Like you and me. They never learn.
And every summer, they return.

Whethering

The rain is haunted;
I had forgotten.
My children are two hours abed
And yet I rise
Hearing behind the typing of the rain,

Its abacus and digits,
A voice calling me again,
Softer, clearer.
The kids lie buried under duvets, sound
Asleep. It isn't them I hear, it's

Something formless that fidgets
Beyond the window's benighted mirror,
Where a negative develops, where reflection
Holds up a glass of spirits.
White noise

Precipitates.
Rain is a kind of recollection.
Much has been shed,
Hissing indignantly into the ground.
It is the listening

Belates,
Haunted by these finger taps and sighs
Behind the beaded-curtain glistening,
As though by choices that we didn't make and never wanted,
As though by the dead and misbegotten.

"LAGNIAPPE" OF

UNCOLLECTED

POEMS

(1999—2017)

Fear of Happiness

Looking back, it's something I've always had:
As a kid, it was a glass-floored elevator
I crouched at the bottom of, my eyes squinched tight,
Or staircase whose gaps I was afraid I'd slip through,
Though someone always said I'd be all right—
Just don't look down or *See, it's not so bad*
(The nothing rising underfoot). Then later
The high-dive at the pool, the tree-house perch,
Ferris wheels, balconies, cliffs, a penthouse view,
The merest thought of airplanes. You can call
It a fear of heights, a horror of the deep;
But it isn't the unfathomable fall
That makes me giddy, makes my stomach lurch,
It's that the ledge itself invents the leap.

Chairs

There are always fewer places than people—
Those are the rules, although you've found
It makes it hard to enjoy the music.
At parties, it's the old classic—

Dance of no partners, round and round.
It makes it hard to enjoy the music
When the tune builds and starts to topple—
The lurch you're left in when the sound

Stops, and suddenly the people
Scramble for what remains. The basic
Principle is not profound.
It makes it hard to enjoy the music—

The carnival feeling, green and awful,
Turning like the revolving ground.
Fewer and fewer places. And people
Pushing and crowding. It makes you sick

And tired. You just want to sit down—
But all of the places are taken by people.
The music stutters. There is no music.

Song: The Rivers of Hell

I know four of them well—
The broad-backed rivers of Hell
Depositing their silt
Of black and fertile guilt.

I know the river Hate,
Its traffic and its freight.
When kindness was in drouth
Its mouth hath been my mouth.

I know the river Woe,
Its tidal undertow,
The way it gulps you down—
A dismal place to drown.

I know the river Burning—
Its twisting and its turning.
When hope of love was fled,
I've tossed upon its bed.

I know the river of Tears—
I've waded it for years.
And I have sipped its brine
In vintages like wine.

The Rivers of Hell in flood
Course through my veins like blood—
I'm intimate with four—
But there's one river more:

Kneeling at its brink,
Still I could not drink
The waters of Forget.
At least, not yet, not yet.

Jack-O'-Lanterns

In retrospect, it seems a bad idea—
We've hardly done it since,
Our party with a theme of booze and knives
To honor ghosts with, as the light got less
And autumn started dropping its dry hints—

Good, dirty fun, scooping the innards out,
The childish entertainment it affords:
Carving of raw faces,
The candle in the basement of the brain
Behind the eyes, lighting the gutted spaces,

Animating zombies out of gourds.
A contest too—why not?—spurring the guests
To dredge their nightmares for those eyes, that leer,
Or some triangulation of cliché
Ripe for the time of year,

Trepanned imagination; but the one
That least affrighted,
So absolutely without thought or art,
Was by the guest that no one seemed to know
And no one could remember who'd invited,

Who'd brought a pumpkin nondescript as he
And simply slashed where others planned and drew:
Two pokes for eyes, one slipping slightly south,
A straight slit for a nose, and then askew—
Slapdash of a mouth.

We hove the dozen pumpkins to the porch
To set twelve grimaces all in a line,
And someone (Bob)
Lanky as an Ichabod in black
And tall as a ladder, who could do the job,

Twisted the bulb out to turn on the dark.
Talk stuttered to a halt as we all stared
At those who stared at us,
None of them exactly as we'd thought,
But other, and themselves, and luminous:

The simplest so expressionless, it seemed
The sallow gawk of horror in the mirror
Before the recognition of the face,
Just as the thing that cannot be undone
Starts getting coldly clearer . . .

It won—anonymous that came alive.
Then Bob, reaching to screw the porch bulb back,
Startled in the socket
A small brown bat that flinched into the air
Ragged as the inside of a pocket,

And everyone gasped a little, and everyone laughed—
A bat seemed blessed
For such a night, as light clicked on and shadow
Drew back to shadow and the moment fled
Unnoticed, like an uninvited guest.

Mosaic Once Depicting Arianist Saints

The marvellous mosaic portraying Theodoric's Palatium . . .
is an accurate representation of the luxurious royal palace . . .
Bishop Agnello (who reintroduced the Catholic faith), eliminated
several of the Arian characters portrayed. Traces of these figures
can still be seen in the white parts of the columns.
—Ravenna guidebook

Glass tesserae in all the hues
Of gilt, unfolding like gold cloth—
Save for the palace of the Ostrogoth,
Where gloom tiles up the porticoes

Once aflame with flashing aether.
We can make out where there were heads—
Ciphers of snuffed-out haloes in their steads,
Like smoke breathed from extinguished fire.

Revision is not absolute—
Two hands that crossed outside an arch
Remain, and shades of feet that used to march
Beneath—the members that refute

Corrections they are tacked onto.
All that is, seen and unseen
Crowds upon us, for what do they mean
Those figures dim in pentimento?

A mosaic is not of one substance.
Made, not eternal. Blue and green,
Like a peacock's iridescent sheen,
Wink with myriad heresies.

The Magi

Christmas Eve, the Word made Flesh,
We put the baby in the manger,
But could not add them to the crèche—
They still had miles of doubt and danger.

They set out from the staircase landing,
Travelling lightly and untrammeled:
One was kneeling, one was standing,
And our favorite was cameled.

Past falling cards and other perils
They crossed the piano's dark plateau
Where someone fumbled Christmas carols
And sang of silence, stars and snow.

They camped wherever they were able,
A potted fern for an oasis.
From shelf to windowsill to table,
Night by night, we'd change their places.

The thrill of our own gifts forgot,
No longer new, the batteries
Gone dead, at last they'd reach the spot,
One king already on his knees,

One kneeling, while the camel grunted—
Twelve whole days of Christmas hence—
To give what no child ever wanted:
Gold and myrrh and frankincense.

After Reading the
Biography *Savage Beauty*

I'd like to write sonnets, a dozen a day,
Compose a libretto and maybe a play.
My lustrous red hair would be crowned with the bay
If I were like Edna St. Vincent Millay.

I'd like to have lovers, both straight ones and gay,
I'd like to hold *both* sexes under my sway
And not give two figs about what people say
Like Edna, Edna St. Vincent Millay.

I'd like to throw tantrums and get my own way,
I'd like to be fresh as a young Beaujolais,
And slyly bewitching as Morgan le Fay,
Like Edna, Edna St. Vincent Millay.

I'd move with the grace of one trained in ballet.
My husband would not only love but obey.
People would flock to my readings—and pay—
If I were like Edna St. Vincent Millay.

Daphne, After

Rooted in my shade so long,
I have forgotten dance, and song,

The wild escape that brought me here.
My hair is leaves, the leaves are sere

And pregnant with a bitter oil,
My grip is pitch-forked in the soil.

No one pursues. I do not run
But stand all seasons in the sun:

Autumn shook me for his rattle,
Winter wooed me. Witless prattle

Coupled in my brain all spring
And changed into a crackled thing.

A poet's wreath, a girl's lost beauty
Crown me dryly, like a duty;

Now that the wind begins to shift,
Careless as a match, and swift,

Let summer find me in his turn
Slow to fade, and quick to burn.

The Barnacle

The barnacle is rather odd—
It's not related to the clam
Or limpet. It's an arthropod,
Though one that doesn't give a damn.

Cousin to the crab and shrimp,
When larval, it can twitch and swim,
And make decisions—tiny imp
That flits according to its whim.

Once grown, with nothing more to prove
It hunkers down, and will remain
Stuck fast. And once it does not move,
Has no more purpose for a brain.

Its one boast is, it will not budge,
Cemented where it chanced to sink,
Sclerotic, stubborn as a grudge.
Settled, it does not need to think.

Learning to Read Greek

As though a host of diacritical marks
Swooped over the rough breathing of the sea,
The swallows parse the brightness in dark arcs,
Glossing the infinitive *to be*.
Hexameters drum surging to the shore,
Spondaic at the end, with their long vowels.
The sea gleams like a shield washed clean of gore,
And as light's noun declines, the little owls
Pipe from the needled forest, each to each,
In dialect, about time's take and give,
The aorist Now forever out of reach,
And how the moon is chaste and has been wronged,
And speak of sorrow in the genitive,
As if it were to her the world belonged.

The Arsenic Hour

The pasta water's on the boil, and I'm
Trying to keep the lid on—have some wine,
I tell myself. Now is when baths are drawn
Like battle-lines, when long-division, fraught
With faux newfangled-ness, must be retaught,
Relearned, resentment for the dividends—
Quotients, remainders—after all, what's time
But long division? Twenty-fours and twelves,
Sixties, sevens, three-hundred sixty-fives,
Fractions in which we parcel our prime selves.
The phone call is impossible, my friends!
Now is the husbandry that falls to wives,
Wrestling the insurgents off to sleep,
The chore that never ends, until it ends,
The work of days, the work that will not keep.

UNCOLLECTED

TRANSLATIONS

Yannis Keats

FROM THE GREEK OF ANGELOS SIKELIANOS

A branch, the hand of Apollo,
The plane tree's polished, broad bough,
Spread above you, may it bring you
The universe's immortal peace.

You'd meet me on the broad and shining shore
      Of Pylos, so I'd planned,
With Mentor's tall ship pulled up on the beach
      Snug in the sand.

We would be bound, as those who sailed with the gods,
      In the winged friendship of youth,
And would take our seats in the stone thrones that Time
      And custom had made smooth

And meet that man who still in the third generation
      Reigned serene, a sage
Whose tales of travels and holy decrees had ripened
      In his mind with age—

At dawn, we'd attend the sacrifice to the gods,
      The ritual slaughters
Of the three-year-old heifers, and hear the single cry
      That rose from his three daughters

When the axe thwacked, and the black-fringed, slow-rolling eye
        Drowned in a swoon
Of darkness, and the gilt horns were rendered idle,
        A hazy half moon.

My love imagined you, as a sister her brother,
        In your virginal bath,
How Polycaste rinsed your naked body and dressed you
        In a robe of fine cloth.

I thought to prod you a little with my foot
        As dawn was about to break:
The gleaming chariot's yoked for us and ready.
        No time to lose! Awake!

And to spend all day in the talk that comes and goes,
        Or silence, when no one spoke,
While we drove the horses who were always leaning one way
        Or another against the yoke,

But most of all I wanted to see your eyes,
        Your deer-like eyes, behold
The palace of Menelaus, and forget themselves
        In bronze and the gleam of gold,

Unwavering gaze, sinking the sight so deep,
        You'd never remember
The figured silver, the ivory, gilded or white,
        The heavy amber,

And I thought that I would say in a hushed voice
        Leaning close to your ear,
Watch out, my friend, because in a moment, soon,
        Helen will appear

Before our very eyes, the one and only
        Daughter of the Swan,
And then we will sink our eyelids in the river
        Of Oblivion.

■

So brightly I saw you; but what grassy roads
        Have led me to your tomb!
And the blazing roses with which I strew your grave
        And make all Rome abloom,

Light the way unto your golden songs
        As though they were the brave,
Armed bodies that turn to dust before one's eyes
        In an ancient, new-breached grave,

And all the worthy treasure of Mycenae,
        The golden plunder
I thought to lay before you—goblet, sword,
        And diadem—past wonder,

A mask on your dead beauty like the mask
        That covered the face
Of the king of the Achaeans—all gold, all artifice,
        Hammered upon Death's trace.

Frieze

FROM THE GREEK OF ANGELOS SIKELIANOS

Kicking their steeds' flanks with the red apples
of their heels, right where the bulging vein
forks and ramifies, and the sweat dripples
in rivulets down to the hooves from the belly,

driving them with palms slapped on the withers
where the hair is parted so the mane
falls on either side like swan feathers,
and crowned themselves with hats or wreaths, they urge

them on—heat splits the earth—the cicada's throb
in the olives heralds airy victory—
here comes the procession, the ceremonial robe;

and then with a fair and following breeze, they surge
past, abounding wave of horses, dancing—
galloping, cantering or prancing . . .

Upon a Line of Foreign Verse

FROM THE GREEK OF GEORGE SEFERIS

to Elli, Christmas 1931

Happy is he who has made the journey of Odysseus. Happy if, as the
    journey loomed,
he felt the sturdy rigging of a love, stretched taut inside his body like
    the veins where the blood boomed.

Of a love with unbroken rhythm, invincible as music and undying,
because it was born when we were born, and whether it dies when we
    do, we do not know, and it is no use trying.

God help me to say, in a moment of great joy, what is this love?
I sit sometimes surrounded by an alien land, and I hear its distant roar,
    like the boom of the sea mingled with an inexplicable whirlwind
    from above.

And again and again, the shade of Odysseus appears before me, with
    eyes red from the brine of the waves, and from a ripe yearning to
    see once more
the smoke wafting from the warmth of his house, and the dog grown
    old waiting at the door.

There he stands, tall, whispering through his whitened beard words
    of our tongue, as it was spoken three thousand years ago.

He holds out a palm calloused from the ropes and the tiller, with skin
    weathered by the dry north wind, by the scorching heat and the
    snow.

It's as though he wants to banish from our midst the superhuman Cy-
    clops, who watches with one eye, the Sirens, whose song makes
    you forget, and Scylla and Charybdis, who swallow you whole,
so many elaborate monsters that keep us from reflecting how he was
    a man who strove in the world, with his body and his soul.

He is the great Odysseus, the one who directed them to build the
    wooden horse, and the Achaeans won Troy;
I imagine he is coming to tell me how to build a wooden horse so I
    may win my own Troy.

Because he speaks humbly and serenely, without effort, he seems to
    know me like a father,
or like the old mariners, who, leaning on their nets, at the hour of
    winter and the wind's anger,

would sing to me in my childhood the song of Erotokritos, with their
    eyes full of tears,
and in my sleep, still thinking of the unjust fate of Arete descending
    the marble staircase, I was seized with fears.

He tells me how hard the pain is, to feel the sails of your ship belly
    with memory and your soul become the helm,
to be alone and rudderless as chaff on the threshing floor, when the
    shadows overwhelm,

the bitterness of seeing your companions sunk into the elements, scat-
  tered, one by one,
and how strange it is to become a man by speaking with the Dead,
  when the Living who remain are no longer sufficient unto you—
  none.

He speaks ... I still see his hands, that knew how to test if the mermaid
  on the prow was well-carven, without splinter,
giving me the unruffled blue sea in the heart of winter.

Acknowledgments

I am grateful to the editors of my previous volumes, including William Baer, Parneshia Jones, and Mike Levine, and to Dana Gioia, who selected *Archaic Smile* for the Richard Wilbur Award. It has also been immensely encouraging to be recognized by the Poets' Prize for *Hapax*, and to be a finalist for the National Book Critics Circle Award with *Olives*, and a finalist for the Pulitzer Prize with *Like*. A special thank-you to Jonathan Galassi, for his keen eye and sympathetic ear with *Like*, and for suggesting I undertake this selected.

I am grateful for many anthologies and composers for picking up some of these verses and giving them new context. In particular, I am honored that so many of these poems have appeared in the Best American Poetry series, edited by David Lehman, including "Apollo Takes Charge of His Muses," from the *Beloit Poetry Journal*, which was perhaps my first published poem as an adult.

I am grateful to Hawthornden Castle for a residency in 2004, where some of these poems were written, and to United States Artists, the Guggenheim Foundation, and the MacArthur Foundation for grants and fellowships that provided moral and practical support.

It occurs to me I have never thanked in writing the woman whose loving childcare and assistance around the house made much of this possible, Tsanka Petkova. Благодаря ти.

Thank you to my husband, John Psaropoulos, who has remained my first reader in sickness and in health and for better or worse through three decades.

I have decided not to tinker with poems that have been previously published; they are the work of a different, earlier me, and it is not my place to alter her work. That said, occasionally I have adjusted a spelling for consistency or corrected for shaky grammar. But other errors I have left alone.

Sometimes there were poems that did not fit into collections because they repeated a subject or form or did not belong thematically. A handful of these, and some translations from modern Greek, I have decided to include here, collecting them for the first time.

"Fear of Happiness" first appeared in *Poetry*

"Chairs" first appeared in *Poetry*

"Jack-O'-Lanterns" first appeared in the *Warwick Review*

"Song: The Rivers of Hell" first appeared in *River Styx*

"The Magi" first appeared in *First Things*

"Learning to Read Greek" first appeared in the *Southern Poetry Review*

"The Barnacle" first appeared in *Poetry*

"The Arsenic Hour" first appeared in *San Diego Reader*

The translation of "Frieze," by Angelos Sikelianos, first appeared in
The New Criterion

The translation of "Upon a Line of Foreign Verse," by George Seferis,
first appeared in *Poetry*

Index of Titles and First Lines

First lines are in plain text.
Titles are in *italics*.